TEACH WITH SUCCESS

Written by
Guy P. Leavitt

Revision and Leader's Guide by
Dr. Eleanor Daniel

Illustrated by
Pat Karch

STANDARD PUBLISHING
Cincinnati, Ohio   3232

Library of Congress Catalog Card No. 78-63285

ISBN: 0-87239-231-7

CONTENTS

Keep It Simple/Make It Fun!

Revision

Unit Two: Teach the Word of God

Unit Three: Evaluate

K-I-S-M-I-F

A boy scout leader attended a training camp, intending to learn how to become a better instructor of boys. He and the others in attendance were mystified by a strange word posted prominently about the camp. The word was KISMIF. The scout leaders asked its meaning, but those in charge merely smiled and said, "Wait and see." The men talked with one another about it, trying to guess what it meant. They were keenly curious. Not until they had been there several days and the training period was half over did they learn the meaning of the word. They were told it was made up of initials to words which contained the secret of all good teaching. The initials K-I-S-M-I-F stood for the words:

KEEP IT SIMPLE
MAKE IT FUN!

This I have tried to do in this book. That is why I have used the second person, singular; why I have utilized half a hundred and more charts, outlines, quizzes and other entertaining devices endeavoring to avoid the academic and strive for readability. I want Sunday-school teachers to read this book and enjoy it! I have tried to bring to it my own experiences and observations in a half-century of teaching and training others to teach in the Sunday school. I am deeply grateful to the thousands of good teachers who have helped.

Guy P. Leavitt

REVISION

I was first introduced to *Teach With Success* back in 1959, when I was a sophomore in college and was assigned to read the book for an assignment in Methods and Techniques of Teaching. But like most college sophomores, I read the book mostly to pass a test—and then promptly put the book on the shelf to be used as a reference now and then through the years.

The years have passed quickly, and my ministry, too, has been the Sunday school—Christian education. Years of formal education and experience contributed to the formulation of a philosophy and practice of teaching. Dozens of teachers' seminars confirmed the needs. Then came the assignment to revise *Teach With Success* which forced me back to a careful reappraisal of my old college text. And an amazing thing happened. Rereading that old text was exciting and enjoyable, for it was almost as up-to-date as the morning newspaper.

Revision has been enjoyable. The chapters have been rearranged—some combined, others expanded, one added. Materials have been expanded where necessary. Some new material was added; dated materials were deleted. But by and large, Guy Leavitt still speaks in his own words to teachers today. He speaks the message well. I trust that a new generation of teachers will be blessed by it!

Dr. Eleanor Daniel

Unit One

PREPARE YOURSELF

CHAPTER 1

KNOW YOURSELF

YOUR CALL

God has bestowed a great compliment upon you. He has called you to teach His Word!

Teaching the Word of God to someone is exciting. The fact that God allows fallible human beings to teach His Word is a privilege beyond measure. The fact that He holds those who teach responsible for a clear, Biblically-sound presentation is a sobering responsibility.

The Bible clearly indicates the responsibility of teaching. Not everyone possesses the gift of teaching, as stated in the New Testament; but everyone does carry the obligation at least to share the Good News with others by presenting a defense of the faith and answering his hope for faith. Paul instructed Timothy, "Be diligent to present yourself approved to God as a workman who does not need to be ashamed, handling accurately the word of truth" (2 Timothy 2:15, *NASB*). Peter instructed, "Sanctify Christ as Lord in your hearts, always being ready to make a defense to every one who asks you to give an account for the hope that is in you, yet with gentleness and reverence" (1 Peter 3:15, *NASB*).

The church of the New Testament attended to teaching. As early as the founding of the church, the Bible states that the new Christians devoted themselves to the apostles' teaching (Acts 2:42). In Acts 6, seven men were selected to perform a specific ministry to the widows because the apostles' priority was prayer and the ministry of the Word. Prophets and teachers were identified in the church at Antioch (Acts 13:1). Christians in Berea examined the Scriptures daily (Acts 17:11) and were, therefore, identified as being more noble-minded than the brethren in Thessalonica.

Paul mentioned the gift of teaching three times in the epistles (Romans 12:7, 1 Corinthians 12:28, Ephesians 4:11). It is listed as a gift of functional service in the church to build up the disciples in the faith and to strengthen

11

the body for ministry and for glorifying Christ. He instructed Timothy, "The things which you have heard from me in the presence of many witnesses, these entrust to faithful men, who will be able to teach others also" (2 Timothy 2:2, NASB). Over and over again, the New Testament imperative rings; the Word of God must be taught by faithful teachers to faithful listeners.

Teaching imposes obligations upon the teacher. Paul instructed Timothy, "Be diligent to present yourself approved to God as a workman who does not need to be ashamed, handling accurately the word of truth" (2 Timothy 2:15, NASB), and he urged Titus, "Speak the things which are fitting for sound doctrine" (Titus 2:1, NASB). The urgency of the responsibility is summed up in James 3:1 (NASB): "Let not many of you become teachers, my brethren, knowing that as such we shall incur a stricter judgment." The teacher is responsible for *what* and *how* he teaches.

Indeed the task of teaching is a big job. But it is God's job. How fortunate you are to share in it!

YOUR QUALIFICATIONS

Who are these teachers? Who is a Sunday-school teacher? The picture of the average teacher may vary from place to place, but some general descriptions may be made.

Teachers come in all ages and sizes and from all kinds of backgrounds and walks of life. In one medium-sized Sunday school in a midwestern metropolitan area, for example, the Sunday-school staff is composed of a lawyer, a music teacher, homemakers, an architect, an engineer, a secretary, and a teacher. Another large midwestern congregation, situated in a small city, has factory workers, college professors, homemakers, secretaries, teachers, businessmen, maintenance supervisors, nursing home administrators, graduate students, paramedics, nurses, and a host of others, teaching God's Word. The average teacher is a person from any walk of life who is committed to Christ and to the church and who wants to have a part in communicating God's Word to a particular age group.

The average teacher has limited formal preparation. And the average teacher teaches in much the same way that he has been taught.

The greatest weakness of the average teacher is not his lack of formal preparation or even his lack of time to do the job as well as a professional teacher. Rather, his greatest weakness is that he is self-satisfied. He doesn't feel any need to improve.

You may be average in many ways, but you are better than average in at least one way. You want to improve. That is the first step. Now take a look at yourself. Decide where you need to improve.

Fortunately, you have the best possible means for comparison and evaluation. You have a divine standard for measuring your qualifications. This standard was established by Jesus, the Christ, the Master Teacher.

Much of Christ's ministry while on earth was devoted to teaching. He referred to himself as teacher. His followers were called disciples, or learners. Even His enemies addressed Him as "Rabbi" or teacher. He was prophet, priest, preacher, and king, but by His teaching He revealed the method by which the world is to be won. He sent His disciples out to teach all nations. In sixty out of ninety times in which Jesus was addressed in the New Testament He was called teacher. If you follow His pattern, your success as a teacher is assured.

Jesus, we are told in Luke 2:52, advanced in four ways: spiritually, socially, mentally, and physically. Suppose, therefore, that you as a teacher consider yourself in all of these aspects.

Spiritually, are you a Christian?

Socially, how well do you get along with people? Are you mature? How about your personality?

Mentally, are you alert and growing?

Physically, do you eat the proper foods, get plenty of rest, exercise, stay away from harmful habits?

Advance In Favor With God

Are you a Christian? This is a blunt question, but it must be asked and answered.

You are not teaching history, geography, or arithmetic. As important as these subjects may be, you are teaching something far more important. You are handling heavenly subject matter.

You are not only training minds, you are developing souls.

Jesus made your position quite clear. The Bible records it this way in Luke 6:39, 40:

> He spoke a parable to them: "A blind man cannot guide a blind man, can he? Will they not both fall into a pit? A pupil is not above his teacher; but everyone, after he has been fully trained, will be like his teacher" *(NASB).*

Jesus knew full well that as a Christian teacher you teach some by what you say and more by what you do. *But you teach most by what you are.*

Your pupils may learn more facts about the Bible than you know. They may surpass your ability to explain the Word. But seldom, if ever, will they become more like God than you do.

It's sobering, isn't it? Of course it is! But it is true. As a fountain cannot rise higher than its source, your teaching cannot be better than you are.

Perhaps you remember a teacher whose Christianity was so apparent that it radiated throughout his life. Even to know him as a friend was to be helped, strengthened, and guided into the way of righteousness. That teacher's love of God, His Son, His Word, His church, as well as his companionship with the Holy Spirit, were so obvious that no one had to tell you that he was a Christian. You may not remember a thing he said, but you remember him. His influence is still a help to you.

That is the kind of a Christian a teacher needs to be. Your Christianity is not judged by the fact that your name is on a church roll as a member. You must be a church member, of course, and a good one; but your Christianity is not verified by this fact alone.

Nor is your Christianity to be validated by your knowledge of creed and dogma. One could know and recite from memory every word in the Bible and still not be a Christian. The devil knows and can quote Scripture as he demonstrated when he tempted Jesus.

You believe in God and in the deity of His Son, Jesus Christ. You treasure your knowledge of the Holy Spirit, and you accept the Bible as God's Word. Important as your faith is, however, it does not mean that you are a Christian. The devil believes, but he is not saved.

Even such outward manifestations as church membership, attendance at all sessions, giving, praying, Bible reading, and irreproachable behavior are not enough. The pupil sees deeper. He sees your personal relationship with Christ. He sees the inner life which cannot be concealed.

May God forgive us if, in a desperate endeavor to encourage better teaching, we give so much attention to methods that we fail to give chief emphasis to the teacher's relationship to Jesus Christ. Let us keep first things first. The best training and the latest methods are but empty gestures, if the teacher is not first a Christian.

So important is this need for the teacher to be a Christian that a consecrated but untrained teacher is to be preferred to the one who is trained but not deeply consecrated. However, you can be both consecrated and trained. That is the ideal.

Probably you have met this first and most important requirement, for most Sunday-school teachers are consecrated Christians. Being Christian teachers already, it should be relatively easy for them to become trained teachers.

To get back to you. Are you a Christian? Earlier we belittled the question-and-answer method of deciding whether one is a Christian. Yet such a method can be indicative. Suppose, therefore, that you answer some questions—not for others to know, but just between yourself and the Lord—regarding your spiritual qualifications as a teacher. Ask yourself:

	Yes	No
Am I an active, supporting member of my local church?		
Do those in my home and at my work consider me to be the kind of Christian I ought to be?		
Do I pray every day?		
Do I read from the Bible every day and meditate upon what I have read?		
Do I make it the rule of my life to attend the services of the church?		
In public, are my dress, words, and general behavior such as bring honor to my Lord?		
Am I thoroughly committed to the Christian work entrusted to me? Am I willing to make the sacrifices necessary for spiritual success?		
In my innermost soul, and before God, am I absolutely sure that I am all that a Christian should be?		

Beware of that final question! It has a catch to it. If you are indeed a Christian, the catch is instantly obvious. Humility and a realization of one's own need for a forgiving Redeemer in the lifelong struggle to measure up to the high calling of being a Christian will mark your attitude.

As a teacher in the church, your purpose is to help others to become Christians and to grow as Christians. How can you do that if you are not a Christian yourself?

No one can teach effectively by depending solely upon the textbook. Behind the teaching materials must be the teacher's vital, growing faith, nourished and disciplined in study, in prayer, and in the practice of the presence of God. For the teacher is not merely imparting a knowledge of the contents of the Bible. He is trying to bring individuals into a saving knowledge of the Lord and an unshakable trust in His will. The basic requirement is that the teacher have a personal faith to communicate. Like Old Mother Hubbard, whose cupboard was bare, if his soul is empty, he has nothing to share. You, the teacher, must seek ever closer communion with God and fellowship with Jesus.

The necessity for the teacher to be a growing Christian cannot be overemphasized. First attention must be given to this qualification.

Don't become discouraged in your efforts to grow. First, you must be aware that you do not always measure up fully to the Christian's standard of thinking and feeling and acting. Along with this awareness of need, you must be firm in your convictions about the authority of the Bible, the living presence of God, the deity of Christ as the Son of God, the power of the Holy Spirit, and the need of every individual, including yourself, for the gospel's antidote for sin. Paul's "all have sinned" (Romans 3:23) includes you.

To grow, expect much of the Lord. Like Paul, you may say, "I can do all things through Christ which strengtheneth me" (Philippians 4:13). But be careful where you put the emphasis when you say this. It is not enough to say, "I can do all things," and slide over the rest, for that is the attitude of the self-sufficient, self-satisfied teacher. Such a teacher does not pray for divine help, does not study to improve teaching technique, and does not love his pupils. He is a failure.

Nor do you say, "I can do all things through Christ," and stop there. The teacher who takes his burden to the Lord and leaves it there before he has done his best to carry it is not being fair to the Lord. To take your burdens to the Lord in prayer is your wonderful privilege as a Christian. In His Word, He tells you again and again that you are to ask, to knock, to seek His help. It is well to take your burden to the Lord and then quit worrying. But here is the point. The growing teacher does not say, "I can do all things through Christ," and stop, putting the emphasis upon the words "through Christ." Christ can do all things; true. But He does not choose to do all things apart from a human instrument. He has enlisted you to be a teacher of His Word to His precious followers. Make yourself available to be the one through whom Christ does all things.

The final phrase of Paul's assertion is needed: "which strengthenth me." You can be a successful teacher if you are a Christian who believes that you can do all things through Christ who is strengthening you. You obviously are not perfect. No teacher, other than Christ, can claim perfection. Yet, as a Christian you can do all things with His help.

Advance In Favor With Men—Get Along With Others

Preparing to teach begins with you. One of the first questions you must answer is this one—how well do you get along with people?

A wise employer, talking to a new employee, gave him this bit of wisdom: "This company expects three things of you. First, you ought to have the ability to do your job. But mere ability is not as important as the other two. We expect you to be honest—not the sort of honesty that keeps you from robbing the till, but honest with yourself, the feeling that you are really interested in your work, that you believe that it is worthwhile. This second requirement is more difficult to meet than the first, but it is not as important as the third. The third is this: We expect you to get along with other people— your fellow employees and people in general. It may surprise you to know that while we can find many employees who have ability, and almost as many who are honest, it is not easy to find one who can get along with other people."

The Sunday-school teacher must be expert at getting along with people. The basic principle in such a relationship was voiced by Jesus when He said, "Thou shalt love thy neighbor as thyself."

The successful Sunday-school teacher is careful to work with his class, his department, his school, his local church, and thus with the Lord himself. If an organization chart were to be drawn up showing the teacher's place in the church, it would show the Lord as head of the church, with the teacher working alongside the minister, elders, and all others who are members of His team.

The teacher cooperates with the pupil, realizing that his place is not to lead or direct, but to accompany the pupil in the learning process. The pupil's interests and opinions are, therefore, given consideration.

The teacher cooperates with the pupil's parents or family, discussing with them the lessons that are to be learned and gaining their assistance.

The teacher cooperates with the other teachers, attending teachers' meetings and sharing experiences and discoveries with his co-workers.

The teacher cooperates with his superintendent, welcoming any suggestions to make the school's efforts more effective.

The teacher cooperates with the minister so that the teaching in the classroom may complement the preaching from the pulpit.

The teacher cooperates with the church's officers, recognizing that the school is a part of the church and is, therefore, directed by the congregation's selected leadership.

The teacher cooperates with the Lord, discussing with Him the details of each lesson, the needs of each pupil, and the effects of the lesson upon the life of each pupil. The Lord is the head of the church and of its school. The teacher is obligated to follow His teachings, His methods, His guidance in carrying out every detail of the work to which He attaches such great importance.

Trite or not, the simple truth is that the Sunday-school teacher's joy is spelled by letting J stand for Jesus first of all in everything, O for others, and Y for yourself last of all. It is also the teacher's rule for finding favor with others. Unselfish devotion to the Lord and to one's neighbor is not only the greatest commandment for the Christian, it is also the soundest of applied psychology.

The Lord's mission was motivated by three great loves: love of God, love of people, and love of truth. "Not as I will, but as thou wilt," was His expression of devotion to the Father. The soul-stirring picture in words, "Jesus . . . was moved with compassion toward them, because they were as sheep not having a shepherd," reveals His love for people.

To advance in favor with man, the teacher unselfishly strives to follow the Lord's example, realizing that good teacher-pupil relationships break down the barriers to the pupil's heart, mind, and will, permitting the seed of the Word of God to find ready and fertile soil. The teacher who does not know how to make friends and influence people is a liability instead of an asset to the Lord's work.

"You ought to come to our class and hear our teacher," is the proud invitation voiced by a man or woman whose teacher knows how to make friends and influence people.

If you teach youth, you can gauge your effectiveness by their confidence in you. When they come to you with their personal problems, like to be in your company, and are proud to be seen with you when you attend their school activities, then you know that you are relating well to them.

A teacher of children wrote, "I recall the thrill that came to me the day Sally saw me coming toward her home. Racing down the steps, she rushed toward me shouting, 'My teacher! My teacher!' Her happy eyes and her smile expressed a welcome that exceeded words." If you are a teacher of children and your pupils greet you like this, then you can say that you know how to get along with children.

The apostle's instruction, "Abstain from all appearance of evil," applies to every Christian, but with multiplied emphasis to you as a Sunday-school teacher. His further warning in the Roman letter that it is good neither to eat nor drink nor do anything that causes another to stumble is given divine weight by the awesome declaration of the Lord: "Whoso shall offend one of these little ones which believe in me, it were better for him that a millstone were hanged about his neck, and that he were drowned in the depth of the sea" (Matthew 18:6). Your preliminary preparation to teach must include a housecleaning in personal behavior.

Your behavior is important in the classroom. If you show consideration and tolerance of the views of others, making those who disagree with you respect and love you, then you can often win them to your way of thinking and doing. You make a lasting impression by the way you handle difficult persons and themes and situations in the classroom. In every such trial you must overcome the temptation to be less than your best. You must reveal a force of character that causes your pupils to admire you and to want to be like you.

Your behavior is also important outside the classroom. A teacher with bad habits and evil companions may think that he is fooling someone, but he isn't. He isn't fooling God, who sees all and knows all. Neither is he fooling his pupils. Nor does the teacher fool himself when he fails to practice what he teaches. Hypocrisy precludes effective teaching and more often than not does lasting harm to the pupil.

Here, as in every other area, Jesus is your example. He lived a life that was the embodiment of His teaching. He could say, "Which one of you convicts me of sin?" (NASB) He could hear His judges say, "I find no fault with this man" and "This man hath done nothing amiss." He could say, "Be ye therefore perfect, even as your Father which is in heaven is perfect," and His life matched those words. The humble human teacher can claim no such perfection, of course, but he can make Jesus his example. He can make it the purpose of his life to strive to do as the Lord would will, combining his own resources with the unfailing strength of Jesus Christ.

When a child says, "I just love my teacher," that teacher has gone only halfway. His responsibility is not only to win the respect and admiration of the pupil, but also to influence the pupil. Much will be said later about methods which will influence students.

For some years, an editor of a nationally circulated magazine of Christian education conducted an annual search for a man and a woman who would be honored as the year's outstanding teachers in Sunday school. It seemed that almost every class wanted to nominate its teacher. "We just love her," or "He is a wonderful teacher," were the comments. When a class expressed a desire to nominate its teacher, the editor sent a list of suggestions telling what the judges would like to know. Was the teacher a Christian in his daily life? How did the teacher get along in his home? In the community? How much had class attendance increased during the past year? If the class was for pupils who might be expected to make such a decision, how many of them had been added to the church during the year? How many of the teacher's former pupils were now active as workers in the church? What had the class done for missions? These and similar questions dug deep at the roots of the teacher's responsibility. As a result, while many classes "just loved" their teachers or thought he or she was "wonderful," when it came to answering the questions and revealing whether or not the teacher had been a real success, the enthusiasm of the majority quickly cooled. While a teacher must win and retain the respect and affection of the pupils, that teacher's influence upon the pupil is the true gauge of his or her success.

Another suggestion to you as a teacher is that you do not take yourself too seriously. Knowing how to laugh and what to laugh at—even yourself upon occasion—is a desirable Christian quality. The teacher who takes himself too seriously and otherwise behaves as one apart from the pupils is building a wall which often shuts out the desire to learn. No effective teacher need fear a good laugh.

There was the teacher of Junior High boys and girls who said that she would continue teaching upon only one condition. This condition was that a certain girl be removed from her class. She could do nothing with the girl who was crude, rude, and generally disrespectful in her conduct. The teacher was persuaded instead to try praying for the girl fifteen minutes each day for two weeks. She soon realized that she did not know enough about the girl to pray for fifteen minutes. This led to a call in the girl's home where the teacher discovered that the pupil was merely eager for attention. Knowing the pupil's background, the teacher became fond of the girl and was able to lead her into such growth that the problem girl later became one of the best teachers in the Sunday school.

This ability to get along with your pupils is not confined to the classroom. There is the social life of your group. This may include anything from a party to a banquet, a trip to a museum or historic site, hikes and ball games, scavenger hunts, hayrides, or picnics. As a Sunday-school teacher you are aware that the Lord can use a party as well as a prayer meeting. Your job will be to help your pupils plan these events, be among the first to arrive and the last to leave, and to see that the good achieved at such affairs is conserved. You must display an interest in the life of your pupils outside the classroom if you want them to be influenced by your teaching.

Needless to add, perhaps, your class knows whether you are finding joy in your teaching. The teacher who approaches Sunday morning with the prayer, "Lord, help me, for this is one of the most wonderful opportunities you have ever given me as Your servant," will enjoy teaching. And a lesson enjoyed is a lesson more likely to be learned.

To summarize the answer to the question of how well you get along with people, check the following:

	YES	NO	PARTLY
I know and speak to each of my pupils by name.			
I have visited in the home of each pupil.			
I always put the interests of my pupils ahead of my own interests or convenience.			
I pray for each pupil by name daily.			
I am always glad to be with my pupils during the week as well as on Sunday.			
My pupils come to me with their personal problems.			
When a newcomer visits our class, I make it a point to call in his home at once.			
Discipline is not a problem in my class.			
Total			

There are eight statements. Count ten for each one checked "yes" and estimate those answered "partly" with a figure one to nine. Add them, and

18

that is your grade. A grade of 70-80 indicates excellent ability to get along with others. A grade of 40-70 is average, indicating need for improvement. A grade of below 40 calls for an immediate self-improvement program.

Said a teacher in a church's school, "I recall vividly a Sunday-school teacher when I was a boy, who set the kind of an example which we could all wish our children to have. She was a radiant personality and a living spirit of Christian joy and faith. Everyone felt good in her presence. I was glad when she found time, along with caring for eight children of her own and two adopted orphan children, to be our Sunday-school teacher and superintendent."

Note the sentence, *"Everyone felt good in her presence."* That is your goal as a teacher.

Advance In Favor With Men—Develop Your Personality

The goal of every Christian teacher is a mature personality which may be used as an instrument to introduce his pupils to the Lord Jesus Christ. Your personality is your own unique interaction of body, mind, and character qualities that make you different from all others.

How important is your personality? Most people relate first to a person, then to the Person. They relate most easily to a winsome personality.

The good news is that your personality can be improved. You can analyze yourself, lay out a plan for improvement, and then set out to make the necessary alteration.

What qualities are desirable personality factors? Few authorities fully agree on a comprehensive checklist. However, almost every authority will accept the factors listed below.

Has a Neat Appearance. Pupils, particularly children, want their teachers to be attractive—clean and neatly dressed.

"A merry heart maketh a cheerful countenance: but by sorrow of the heart the spirit is broken," is a proverb particularly true of the Sunday-school teacher. The Christian life is a joyous one. Therefore, the Christian teacher is not a sour-faced, patiently pious and sacredly solemn individual, but is one who smiles. Eugene Fields' advice is true:

"Herein the only royal road to fame and fortune lies:

Put not your trust in vinegar—molasses catches flies!"

The sincere smile which accompanies the teacher's greeting is contagious. It uplifts and reassures the pupil and encourages him to be responsive. It reflects a desired atmosphere for the classroom. This does not mean that the teacher has to be a hilarious, backslapping jokester. He is to be temperate in all things including appearance.

Is Enthusiastic. James A. Garfield, Christian minister who was President of the United States, once said, "See to it that you do not serve your pupils with cold victuals. . . . Serve them hot and steaming, and your pupils will have an appetite for your instruction." Your aim as a teacher is to set each pupil on fire to translate what he has learned into an ardent Christian life. To start a fire you must have fire. Your passion should be to win for Christ just as many pupils as you can get into your class, then build them into earnest, working Christians who will remain faithful until death.

Communicates to both intellect and emotions. The effective Bible teacher must be interested in more than simple transmission of facts. Some teachers become so preoccupied with facts that they forget that the final goal of effective Bible teaching is changed behavior by the pupils. Achievement of

changed behavior requires not only feeding the intellect, but also appealing to the emotions.

Likes people. Pupils readily spot teachers who like people. They as easily spot those teachers who don't like people. A great gulf exists between a class and the teacher who doesn't genuinely like them. But a teacher who does genuinely care for his pupils breaks down a multitude of barriers to learning. Very little happens in Christian teaching apart from personal relationships.

Exhibits a healthy sense of humor. The effective teacher knows how to laugh. He permits others to laugh as well.

Perseveres. You will want to quit at times—especially on those days when nothing goes quite right. Your pupils won't always listen. Some will seldom be receptive. You will wonder if teaching is really worth all of your investment of time and energy. It is then that your perseverance is tested. If you have learned to persevere in the small tasks, then you will conquer teaching as well.

Fortunately, you have a model. Jesus is forever the Master Teacher. His example is your pattern. Christ knew human nature. He knew the individual's possibilities as well as his weaknesses. No better advice for improving your personality can be given than this: Pattern yourself after Jesus in all things.

To help you get started toward personality improvement, try this self-test. By making such an analysis you may discover some weaknesses which can be corrected.

PERSONALITY PROFILE TEST
For the Sunday-school Teacher

Quality	Definition	My Estimate		
		Low	Average	Superior
Sincerity	Being true or genuine.			
Dependability	Being faithful, reliable, prompt.			
Enthusiasm	Being intensely interested and earnest.			
Cooperation	Being able to work with others.			
Self-confidence	Feeling sure your ability is equal to the demands.			
Personal Appearance	Being well-groomed, properly presentable in dress and cleanliness.			
Forcefulness	Being decisive; not hesitant.			
Emotional Stability	Being able to maintain poise at all times.			
Tactfulness	Saying and doing what is suitable.			
Courtesy	Being polite, kind, considerate.			
Friendliness	Being cordial.			
Perseverance	Being able to continue effectively in spite of adverse circumstances.			
Patience	Being willing to repeat, restate, and redo in order to help the pupil understand.			
Use of Good English	Using words clearly and understandably.			
Voice Quality	Having a pleasing voice strong enough to be heard but not irritating.			

Advance in Wisdom

Dr. Arthur Holmes asserted that the human brain is capable of doing fifty thousand times more than is asked of it. To settle into a mental rut and stay there is fatal to the success of the Sunday-school teacher. The growing teacher is constantly adding to his storehouse of information, gleaned from wide reading and careful thinking. He must do this if he is to nourish the expanding intellectual life of his pupils. Like a bridge or an elevator which must be capable of supporting a far greater load than it is usually called upon to bear, a teacher's knowledge ought to extend far beyond the demands made upon it. Teachers need to read more.

The conscientious teacher is always learning. The daily newspaper contains valuable information. A walk down the street enriches understanding of human nature. He finds the Bible to be the greatest textbook ever written. As the teacher reads it, he adds the knowledge which he has gained in other reading, observation, and experience.

As a teacher remember this: you make your appeal to your pupil in terms of the whole man—his intellect, as well as his emotions and his will. Through his mind you appeal to his nature. To do this, you must know as much as you can about him and the things in which he is interested. You must be able to "talk his language."

Be careful, though, and don't let your general knowledge interfere with your teaching. Who hasn't heard a teacher say, "I've been reading the most interesting book this week," and then tell about the book without giving the poor pupil a chance to learn anything. It reminds me of a teacher who had visited the Holy Land and couldn't recover from it. She was always dragging in experiences and observations which were not only unrelated to the lesson, but were boresome as well. One lesson had a reference to Jacob's well. She spent the entire lesson period telling of the well, how deep it was, how old it was, how it was made, what it looked like to her when she saw it, and how it differs from other wells both here and abroad. Perhaps it would be a fine thing if every Sunday-school teacher could visit the Holy Land, but not unless the teacher knows how to use the knowledge better than this one did.

You as a teacher must be intellectually alert because you have such a short time in which to teach. In one year your pupils spend less time in Bible study class than the equivalent of two weeks in public school. If a public school teacher were asked to do a year's work of English literature, or social studies, or math in two weeks, he would declare it to be impossible. Yet you, as a Sunday-school teacher, are asked to teach the Bible, Christian history, Christian doctrine, and an understanding of the relation of the Christian faith to all things in life, and do it in those few, brief hours!

Intellect and education do not mean the same thing. Your intellectual ability is natural. If you have even an ordinary mind, it can be developed to a high degree. Education, however, is not natural; it is acquired. You acquire knowledge by study, research, and experimentation. This is education. To be mentally capable as a teacher you are to develop your intellectual ability and add to your knowledge.

Wisdom is more important to you as a teacher than either intellectual ability or knowledge. Wisdom is the quality or state of being wise. It is knowledge of what is true or right coupled with just judgment as to action. Proverbs 4:7 suggests that wisdom is the principal thing. A synonym for wisdom is common sense. A Sunday-school teacher ought to have good, sound common sense.

No sooner was Jonah precipitated into the circumfluent brine than he was ingested by a massive aquatic vertebrate.

A good evidence of wisdom is a person's attitude. If he is wise, he does not become upset over trifles. Instead, he has control of his words, actions, and attitudes. The wise individual can be noticed in any group at once. He is the self-controlled person, well balanced, sure of himself, the "natural leader." The common afflictions of envy, jealousy, self-pity, and intemperance are not permitted to abide in his heart. If you are to be an effective teacher, you must strive to be wise. The best way to do this is to pattern yourself after Jesus, to study Him, and to walk in His steps. "What would Jesus do?" is a good question to answer before you take action.

Careful Bible study, meditation, and much prayer will help you to achieve wisdom. You need to acquire as much education as possible, along with the common sense to use it wisely.

There have been teachers who sought to impress their classes by a pompous parade of their learning. They march out an array of high-sounding phrases beyond the comprehension of their pupils, utter solemn platitudes in a wise tone, and thus boast of extensive study and profound information which mean nothing to the pupil. But what God wants is a teacher who is growing in knowledge and in the common sense of conveying that knowledge to others.

It's not up to you to prove that you have the education needed to be a teacher. You don't have to prove that. Your pupils will know. But it is up to you to use wisely the knowledge that you do have. Your pupils assume that you know enough to teach or you would not be their teacher. Your responsibility is to justify their confidence in you.

It may help you to realize that your teaching is even more important than that of a teacher in the public school.

1. *Your purpose is more important.* The public school helps the pupil to live a better life on this earth. You help him to live both here and hereafter.

2. *Your source material is more important.* The Bible is the world's most important textbook. It is the Word of God, the revelation of His will, His special message for us.

3. *Your responsibility is greater.* If a teacher in the public school fails to help a pupil to learn, the pupil pays the penalty only during this lifetime. If *you* fail, your pupil may be lost eternally.

My Mental Checklist

	Yes	No
I believe that I must educate myself in whatever ways I can to be an effective teacher.		
I believe that the teacher who ceases to learn ceases to teach acceptably. Therefore, as a teacher, I must continually increase my knowledge of the Bible, of my pupils, of teaching techniques, of "readin,' 'ritin,' and 'rithmetic," and of history, science, politics, business, and current subjects.		
I can explain the difference between intellect, education, and wisdom.		
My grammar is above reproach.		
I study the interests which concern my pupils so that I may "talk their language."		
Although I respect public-school teachers, I believe that my work is more important than theirs and that I ought to be as well educated as they are.		
Academic training is not as important as spiritual living in my success as a Sunday-school teacher, but I ought to have both.		
My pupils respect my educational standing.		
I am wise in making use of the knowledge which I have.		

22

YOUR REWARD

What rewards may you expect as a teacher? Exceptional opportunities for individual growth and personal satisfaction are offered to you. Some of these are immediate and material. The growing teacher is rewarded with increasing ability to meet and influence people, to take an expanding place in the home, church, and community, and to understand and do the will of God.

You deal with people. Those who fail in business and industry, as well as in social life, are usually those who are not successful in dealing with people. The teacher's experience, therefore, is a training that makes for progress in other walks of life. Just as one who drives an automobile develops successful procedures into habits, you as a teacher have a superior opportunity to develop the art of getting along with others—to acquire skill in dealing with people.

You learn the Bible. Whether every pupil in the class really learns anything from a lesson may be open to question, but whether the teacher learns cannot be doubted. The best way to learn a subject is to teach it effectively, for the teacher must not only know more than the pupil, but he must know it better. Normally, in every Sunday-school class the subject matter to be presented to the pupils is accurately specified in the teacher's book with a more limited presentation in the pupils' workbook or leaflet. The teacher's duties, however, demand additional related knowledge not found in a quarterly. This background knowledge gives you, the teacher, an ever-increasing grasp of the most precious subject matter in the world, the Word of God.

You become self-confident. Every teacher may be "scared to death" the first time he faces a class, possibly even for months thereafter. This is a good indication. It shows that the teacher is taking the position seriously, recognizing the importance of the responsibility to be fulfilled. As the teacher learns to deal with people and increases in mental development, spiritual growth, and technical knowledge of teaching, he gains in self-confidence. You grow in self-assurance and capability of leadership.

You are appreciated. If you are a capable teacher, you receive a reward that is more than a paycheck. This reward comes in various ways. It may be the word of appreciation from a parent, the superintendent, or the minister; a look of approval on the face of a student; evidence of exceptional interest from the class; or that inward feeling that needs no voice to say, "Well done, thou good and faithful servant."

You know your worth. You perform a vital function in the church. The minister, the soloist, the choir director, and others may occupy a place of prominence before the entire congregation, but you know that it is in the classroom, or in personal contact, in the grass-roots training of the Christian individual that progress is made. When a new convert comes out of the world and into the Lord's kingdom, if that convert is from your class, you need no public announcement of your achievement. Your part in the work of the Lord's team is heralded by the joy that springs from the heart.

You accept a personal challenge. The teaching mission is vital. The job is indispensable. It is the teacher's responsibility. Others are depending upon you: parents, the superintendent, the minister, the church—and the Lord.

You lead people to Christ. Some will be introduced to Christ first in your Bible class. Others will be confronted with areas where they need to grow to maturity. Whichever it is, your reward is to see your pupils come to Christ and grow to maturity and to know that you had a significant part in it.

You are laying up treasure. Your treasure is being laid up both on this earth and in Heaven. On this earth, it is in the growing appreciation of those who learn from your teaching. In Heaven, it is the affirmation of God, for "they that turn many to righteousness (shall shine) as the stars for ever and ever" (Daniel 12:3).

The Sunday-school teachers of America stand at the gateway of the future. The presence of these men and women, who each week prepare to go before classes and interpret some portion of the Word of God, is of more value to this country than all of its other resources. Unsalaried and unsung, they serve because they know it is an honor and a privilege to be a Sunday-school teacher.

CHAPTER 2

KNOW YOUR PURPOSE

What is your purpose as a Sunday-school teacher?

Before you answer that question, one fact must be made clear. Your class is part of the Sunday school. The Sunday school is a part of—not apart from—the church. The church's purpose, therefore, is the purpose of the Sunday school. Your school's purpose is your purpose. Got it? Do you agree?

Speaking to a group of Juniors about the church, a leader asked the question, "What is the church?" The boys and girls had a great time answering. One said that the church is the building with a steeple. True, said the leader, we call the building the church, but is it really the church? Another boy said it was the church service. Yes, the leader agreed, we speak of going to church and we mean that we are going to a particular service. But is that the church? Finally, one little girl answered, "People." And that was the correct answer.

The church is the body of Christ, but this body is made up of people. It is composed of a "peculiar people," that is, people who are different from those around them.

This difference is that they are baptized believers in Christ as the divine Son of God. We call them church members. But, as was explained to the Juniors, this definition is not complete. The church is made up of people who are baptized in Christ—and who are busy at work carrying out His instructions. One must be a worker for Christ if he is to be a Christian.

The church, then, is a body of believing, obedient workers for Christ.

What is this work which He wants His body, the church, to do? It is the purpose of the church, of the Sunday school, of you as the teacher. What is it?

The Lord sums up the work of the church in what is known as the Great Commission. A commission is a task committed to one's charge. The Great Commission is the work committed to you and to me. It is given in Matthew 28:19, 20; Mark 16:15, 16; Luke 24:47, 48; Acts 1:8. It is most complete as given in Matthew:

"Go ye therefore, and teach all nations, baptizing them in the name of the Father, and of the Son, and of the Holy Ghost: Teaching them to observe all things whatsoever I have commanded you."

Notice that it is a two-fold commission. Two tasks are mentioned. Both involve teaching.

Jesus said: "Teach . . . baptizing." This is the teaching of evangelism. You are to recruit for Christ.

He then said: "Teaching them to observe all things whatsoever I have commanded you." This is the teaching of nurture. After we have recruited, or converted one to Christ, we are then to teach him how to grow as a Christian.

When W. C. Pearce, a Christian educator of another generation, was closing what proved to be his last message to the teachers and other workers of the First Christian Church Sunday School in Canton, Ohio, he said with prophetic emphasis: "If this were my last message to this great congregation of Christians, and if I had only three more words to say, those words would be: 'Teach, teach, teach!' "

Jesus, in His final appearance to His followers on this earth, gave His final message in two words. They were: "Teach . . . teaching."

You are the teacher. To carry out the Lord's commission is your purpose. To repeat—this broad goal is twofold.

Purpose No. 1: "Teach all nations, baptizing them," is the teaching of evangelism. The teacher is an evangelist. As a teacher you have the responsibility of trying to win to Christ every pupil in your class. Not only that, but you are to "teach all nations." You are to go beyond your present class. The teacher is to be a class builder, trying to get as many as possible into the class so they can learn about Jesus and accept Him as their Redeemer and Lord. Then they in turn go out to win others.

"But wait," you say, "I teach small children. How can my teaching be evangelistic in purpose?" That is a good question. You need to see evangelism in its broadest scope. Teaching for evangelism means to build, line upon line, precept upon precept, attitude upon attitude, until an individual comes to a personal faith in Jesus Christ and decides to commit his life to Him. Teachers of young children are building the informational and attitudinal foundations which will come to completion in later years.

The teacher of children and youth also have another evangelistic opportunity. He has in his class students whose parents are not Christians. Therefore, his calls and teaching in the pupils' homes are for the purpose of evangelizing not only the pupil, but his family members as well.

Purpose No. 2: "Teaching them to observe all things whatsoever I have commanded you" is the teaching of nurture. The teacher is a conservationist. It is one thing to win a pupil to Christ; it is another task, and an equally important one, to build that pupil into a lifetime Christian. The teacher is expected to do both.

This statement of your two-fold purpose is simple and easy to understand, and it is Biblical. In your reading or listening to speakers, you may hear about the controversy between those who place education above theology, experience above dogma, and those who argue for a social-centered curriculum or a Bible-centered curriculum. This is best illustrated by the story of two men who were arguing. One insisted that he was a Bible-believing Christian. The other claimed to be a Bible-living Christian. For years the Christian educators battled over this question, and the work of the Sunday school was harmed.

The sensible position is that Christian education is both theological and educational. It is both spiritual and social. The teacher's function is to produce Christians who are both Bible-believing and Bible-living.

Indeed, you have a special divine appointment to your task. Writing to the church at Corinth (1 Corinthians 12:28), Paul said: "God hath set some in the church, first apostles, secondarily prophets, thirdly teachers." This puts you high on the list of God's chosen workers in His program for the church.

As a teacher, you have a divine commission, a special assignment, a tremendous responsibility, and a heavenly opportunity. Now let us consider the two parts of your purpose.

YOU ARE TO EVANGELIZE

You are to be an evangelist. You are to convert sinners. To do this means that you are to be a salesman for Christ.

As a soul-winning salesman you need to meet three vital requirements:

1. First, *you must have a personal assurance of your own salvation.* In other words, you must believe what you teach. This means that you must be prepared to tell others in "meekness and fear" how you account for the hope that is in you (1 Peter 3:15). For this hope must first be in your own heart before you can pass it along to others. That is why, at the very beginning of this book, much was said about your own spiritual life.

2. Having a personal assurance of your own salvation, *you next must have a consciousness that people are lost in sin.* You are to believe with all your heart that "there is none righteous, no, not one" (Romans 3:10) and that "all have sinned, and come short of the glory of God" (Romans 3:23).

3. Assured of your own salvation and convinced that everyone is lost and needs a Savior, *you must have faith in Christ as the only Redeemer of man* (John 14:6) and that His purpose in coming to this earth was to seek and to save the lost (Luke 19:10).

Let us compare these Scriptural teachings with the teachings of salesmanship. Suppose that instead of being a salesman for Christ, you were a salesman for an automobile agency. Your job is to sell a certain kind of automobile.

First, you would learn about the product—the automobile. You would become enthusiastic about it. You would drive one when you went to call upon a customer. "I know what it will do," you would say. "I drive one myself."

Next, you would learn about the market. Who needs an automobile? Where are customers to be found? Your market would be limited to those who need an automobile like yours and who have the money to pay for it. (As a salesman for Christ, your market is unlimited. Everyone needs Him. No one needs money, or health, or position, or education to obtain Him. God's grace is free to whosoever will accept it.)

Third, as an automobile salesman, you must be convinced that your automobile is the one your prospective customer needs. There are many makes of automobiles. While everyone agrees that an automobile is practically a necessity, not all agree to use the same kind of automobile. Suppose, however, that yours was the only automobile available, that anyone wanting an automobile had to use yours or go without. That is your situation as a Sunday-school teacher. Jesus is the only Savior. Your purpose, therefore, is to teach the pupil that he is a sinner and that he is condemned to eternal death; that he can be saved; that Jesus Christ is the Son of God; and that Jesus Christ came to save him.

Now that you are assured of your own salvation and convinced that all have sinned and Christ is the only Savior, where do you begin as an evangelist?

Begin Recruiting

1. *In your own class.* If your pupils are old enough to make such a decision, you are to win them to Christ and to active participation in the local congregation. If they are under the age of accountability for their sins, your responsibility is to teach them to know God as Father, Jesus as His Son, and the other facts of Scripture. From the earliest age, the pupil is to be considered as an evangelistic prospect.

2. *In the homes of your pupils.* Parents, brothers, sisters, and other relatives of every pupil are prospects. As the teacher you do not teach them directly, but through your pupil you win them to the church.

3. *Among the friends of your pupils.* Again, your influence as a teacher is not direct, but indirect. Your responsibility is to train your pupil in evangelism.

4. *The community.* Your evangelistic field is your community. As a teacher, you are responsible, with the others in your Sunday school, for making yours a Christian community.

5. *The world.* Your evangelistic influence beyond the local field is expressed by giving your pupils an understanding of missions, of their responsibility for helping win the world to Christ, and of leading them in expressional missionary activity.

As a teacher, how do you carry out this divine responsibility to be an evangelist who recruits for Christ?

Carry Out Your Responsibility

1. *By your teaching.* You are to "teach for a verdict." Every lesson, whether you teach four-year-olds or adults, must have an application.

Suppose, for example, that you are assigned to teach a lesson from Genesis 12:1-9—the call of Abram. You need to examine the passage to learn the facts, of course. But more than that, you need to determine how the facts can be applied evangelistically to your class.

The emphasis for children would be obedience. God wants us to obey whatever He asks us to do. At this age, you will be working to create attitudes of receptivity to doing what God asks of us.

Juniors would also examine the concept of obedience. You would undoubtedly want to emphasize the "blessed to bless" of 12:2. Why are we blessed? How are we blessed? How can we bless others? Each question relates to the fact that God wants to save His people who then will bless others by helping them to know God too.

Teens and adults will examine the same concept as Juniors, but in greater depth. The same three questions must be answered. Those who aren't Christians will be challenged to obey by accepting Christ. Those who are Christians will be challenged to obey by sharing Christ with others.

Even an Old Testament narrative account then has an evangelistic application. When you once come to appreciate the importance of making every lesson a soul-winning experience for the pupil, you will not find difficulty in making this kind of emphasis.

2. *By your prayers.* As the teacher, you are personally concerned about every pupil in your class. You need to keep a notebook, with pages devoted to information about each pupil. Your prayers are to be for these pupils, particularly for those who have not accepted and obeyed Christ. Name them individually in your appeal. Become so deeply concerned about them that you cannot rest until they are in a right relationship with God. That is your responsibility.

3. *By talking with the pupils.* Counseling is one of your most effective methods of teaching. Personal, confidential, conversational instruction is most effective. Generalities in the lesson can be specifically applied in conversation. Until you can talk intimately, sincerely, and helpfully with each pupil about his soul's welfare, you have not achieved your full ministry as a teacher of that pupil. Nor have you measured up to your purpose as a teacher in the Sunday school.

4. *By cooperating with the church's evangelistic program.* Most congregations follow a practice of emphasizing evangelism at special times such as during a period of visitation or "revival" meetings. In these efforts your help is most important. You can provide the workers with a list of the unsaved in your class or the unsaved in their homes or among their friends. You can pray for those of your own class who have not yet decided for Christ, and you can talk with them about the importance of making the right decision. You can even accompany them as they take the step, lending them the influence of your encouragement, your concern, and your love.

Historically, the Sunday school has been the church's most effective evangelistic arm. When churches fail to emphasize the Sunday school, evangelism falters. When churches emphasize the Sunday school, evangelism flourishes. Some churches report that as many as four out of five converts come into the church through the Sunday school.

What makes the Sunday school the church's most important agency of evangelism? Here are some good reasons.

1. Children grow up in the Sunday school and into the church.

2. It is in childhood and youth that most converts are gained. Three out of every four church members make the decision to follow Christ before the age of twenty-one. Chances are three to one that the person who has not accepted Christ by the time he or she reaches the age of twenty-one will never be added to the church. The great waves of conversion come from ten to fifteen years of age.

3. Every pupil is a recruiter, bringing others into the Sunday school and thus into the church.

4. The atmosphere of the Sunday school offers the newcomer a natural step into the more dignified customs of the formal worship service.

5. The teacher who is carrying out the Lord's orders is consecrated and trained to lead the pupils into a saving knowledge and acceptance of His will.

YOU ARE TO NURTURE FOR CHRIST

Having brought the pupil to a saving knowledge of Jesus Christ, your continuing purpose as a teacher is "teaching them whatsoever I have commanded." This is the teaching of nurture. You are to recruit for Christ. Then you are to retain for Christ.

Look at your class next Sunday and remember that three out of five of your pupils may be lost to the church and to Christ before they die. That is the average loss in the Sunday school.

Consider the adults in your community who do not attend church. Seven out of ten of them were at one time regular in church attendance.

Why this loss? It is because we have not realized the importance of the second purpose Christ has assigned to us. We recruit and then forget. We welcome them at the church front door, but disregard them as they disappear through the back door.

Richard Crabtree, minister at First Christian Church, Canton, Ohio, observes that new converts will never grow as Christians should unless they are involved in a Sunday-school class. Therefore, he insists that adult Sunday-school classes are as essential as classes for children.

Your responsibility as a nurturer is as important as your work of evangelism. It isn't enough to bring the pupil to a saving knowledge of Christ. You must keep him there.

Paul outlines this work of nurture in the fourth chapter of the Ephesian letter, verses 12-16. Having spoken of your ministering gift as a teacher, he outlines the purpose of that gift. Let's see what he says:

"For the perfecting of the saints" (v. 12). The convert is a saint. Your responsibility is to make him perfect.

"For the work of the ministry." You are to encourage your pupils to find their own places of service, whatever those may be. The work of ministry may be teaching a class, making a call, listening to the troubled, sponsoring a youth group, or any one of many areas of service in a local congregation. Or it may be encouraging others to be preachers or some other area of specialized service. When O. A. Trinkle was minister of Englewood Christian Church in Indianapolis, he spoke of the Sunday-school teacher who led him to become a minister. "I shed tears of gratitude every time I remember her," he said.

"For the edifying of the body of Christ." The body of Christ is the church, and the members of that body are the members of the church. Your responsibility is to teach them. Every member of the church ought to be in the Sunday school, either teaching or being taught. If one thinks he knows the Bible, he ought to be teaching it to others. If he thinks he has anything to learn from the Bible, he ought to be studying it, either as a teacher or a pupil.

"Till we all come in the unity of the faith" (v. 13). Christian unity is one of the greatest goals of our time. Your responsibility as a teacher is to promote Christian unity by teaching what the Bible has to say, not what men have to say.

"Unto the measure of the stature of the fulness of Christ." Do you teach your pupils to be like Christ?

The next point is one you may have overlooked. With more than two hundred denominations dividing Christ's church in the United States today, and more being added all of the time, Paul tells you that your purpose is to teach "that we henceforth be no more children, tossed to and fro, and carried about with every wind of doctrine, by the sleight of men, and cunning craftiness, whereby they lie in wait to deceive" (v. 14). Your pupils are to know what they believe and why they believe it.

By your "speaking the truth in love" (v. 15), your pupils "may grow up into him (Christ) in all things." Here is the ethical and social training the pupil gains under your teaching—how to behave himself as a Christian.

But this is not all. Perhaps the most important verse is the next one (v. 16) in which Paul speaks of your pupil being fitted and joined as a part of the effectual working functions of the church. He is to become a worker in the church. Your part is to teach him that he is to be a worker, what he is to do, and how he is to do it.

How are you to build the Christian character of your pupils? How can you keep them faithful? How are you to conserve your pupils for Christ? Help them build strong Christian characters? Help them grow?

This book is intended to help you answer those questions. In a general way, so you may comprehend this part of your purpose and its fulfillment, here are some suggestions:

Stop the Leaks. By your example and other teaching. By providing the best classroom and equipment possible. By encouraging an optimistic Christian spirit. By checking every absentee quickly. By making every session interesting and worthwhile. By rewarding faithfulness.

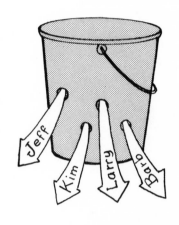

"Use me or lose me." Your pupil must be led to feel that he is an important person. He must be given something to do, both during the class session and outside the class. The teacher who does it all, without letting the pupil participate, is not only failing to teach, but he is also helping to drive the pupil away by robbing him of his interest in the class and the Sunday school. Even the youngest pupil can be made to feel that he has something to do that will help in the Lord's work.

Attend Worship. As a worker in the church, and not only in its Sunday school, you can help strengthen the faith and Christian character of your pupils by teaching them to attend the worship services. Your own attendance and your teaching that such attendance is expected will encourage the pupil to attend. If yours is a group of teenagers, the pupils may benefit by sitting together during the worship service. If you teach a children's group, then graded worship or the extended session is recommended.

Personal Guidance. Pupils need help in selecting books, magazines, and other literature which will nurture their spiritual growth. Why not set up a display of good reading materials in your classroom? (Younger age groups can find them in learning centers.) Brief mention of wholesome movies and television programs will also benefit your pupils.

Just what do you hope to accomplish by teaching next Sunday? To evaluate your understanding of your purpose as a teacher, check the following questions.

MY WORK OF EVANGELISM

	Yes	No
Can I quote the Lord's words setting forth the purpose of my work as a teacher?		
Am I deeply concerned about the salvation of others as demonstrated by the fact that I have talked with at least one person within the last month about accepting Christ?		
Do I know which pupils in my class are unsaved?		
Has my class increased its enrollment by at least ten per cent during the past twelve months?		
Do I aid in a personal calling program, endeavoring to enlist new members of the church and the Sunday school?		
Am I interested in home and foreign missions to the extent that I support them financially and urge my class to support them?		
Do I do all that I can to help my congregation's vacation Bible school?		
Do I make it my aim to emphasize the evangelistic application of every lesson I teach?		

MY WORK OF NURTURE

	Yes	No
Do I promptly follow after every pupil absent from my class in an effort to bring him back to regular attendance?		
Do I have a plan for encouraging my pupils to attend every Sunday?		
Am I careful to emphasize the doctrinal application in every lesson I teach?		
Am I thoroughly familiar with Christian doctrine?		
Do I encourage my pupils to attend the services of the church regularly?		
Am I as deeply concerned about the nurtural development of my pupils as I am about their factual instruction?		
Do I definitely encourage each pupil to read and study for his own self-development?		
Do I definitely encourage each pupil to undertake some church work activity for which he seems best fitted?		
Am I thoroughly familiar with the home life of each pupil? With his social, school, or work interests?		
Do I make it a point to keep in touch with each former pupil, particularly if he has moved from the community?		
Checking back over my pupils of the past, can I say that I succeeded in helping each one of them to grow into an active, faithful Christian?		
Can I conscientiously say that I fully appreciate the importance of my place as a teacher in the Sunday school?		
Total		

A grade of seventy-five per cent, or fifteen "yes" checks, will indicate a promising situation; fifty to seventy-five percent, that improvement will be an easy undertaking; below fifty percent, you have an emergency on your hands.

CHAPTER 3

KNOW YOUR PUPILS

WHAT DO YOU KNOW ABOUT YOUR PUPILS?

Teacher, do you know your pupils? Let's see. Answer these questions below about one person in your class.

Name: _____

Address: _____ Telephone: _____

Date of Birth: _____ Date of Spiritual Birth: _____

Family Members: _____
_____

Interests: _____
_____

Special Abilities: _____
_____

Needs: _____
_____

Educational Background: _____
_____

Service to Christ: _____
_____

Specific Evidences of Christian Growth: _____
_____

Are you sure that you know him? Maybe you do. Maybe you don't. But if you are to teach successfully, you must get to know your pupils personally and specifically.

Each pupil in a class is very much like the other pupils in many ways, but quite different in other ways. You must learn what to count on as unchanging behavior among your pupils and what is quite flexible.

All of this knowledge of your individual pupils is not just an option, something to acquire if it is convenient. It is a must. The pupils' interests, abilities, and experiences are the launching pad for new learning. A good teacher always begins with his pupils where they are, then takes them to where they need to be. He recognizes the necessity of choosing his content, learning activities, and applications to meet the needs of his class members.

An effective teacher knows theology—the revelation of God to man. But he also knows psychology—the explanation of the behavior of man. And he knows pedagogy—the techniques of assisting an individual to learn the content.

A teacher deals with a specific age group—twos, third graders, collegians, or older adults. Twos differ from third graders who differ from collegians who differ from older adults. The teacher plans for a specific age group.

Twos share some things in common as do third graders as do collegians as do older adults. But for everything they share in common, they possess that many unique traits and characteristics which interact with their own environment, socioeconomic status, educational background, and a variety of other factors, to produce their behavior. In short, then, a teacher never teaches a class—he always teaches individuals.

How can you get to know the individuals who comprise your class? The methods vary, of course:
—Observe the reactions of the pupils in the classroom.
—Visit the pupil's home.
—Observe the pupil at work/play/school.
—Interview family members of the pupil.
—Self-evaluation by the pupil.
Get to know your pupils. Then teach to meet their needs.

WHO ARE YOUR PUPILS?

Your pupils are probably grouped by age. Most Bible schools follow a grouping procedure similar to this.

Crib Babies	birth to age one
Toddler	age 1
Twos and Threes	ages 2 and 3
Beginner	ages 4 and 5
Primary	grades 1 and 2
Middler	grades 3 and 4
Junior	grades 5 and 6
Young Teen	grades 7-9
Senior High	grades 10-12
Young Adult	ages 18-24
Adult	ages 25 and above

Because your class will include pupils within a limited age range, there are some things very much alike about them. But there are as many unique characteristics as there are pupils in the class.

Your teacher's book will give you a great deal of help in learning how to meet the needs of your class. It is written by a writer who is experienced in teaching the age level for which the material is intended. The writer takes into account those nearly-universal characteristics, but also suggests ways to enable you to meet the unique factors present in your class. At the same time, however, the teacher must alter the teacher's book where necessary, for no writer will reach everyone of your pupils in detail.

THE METAMORPHOSIS OF A PUPIL

Pupils change, sometimes, it seems, overnight. Take a Junior High boy, for example. You think you know him, and you probably do. He is loud and boisterous. He dislikes girls. Whatever contact he has with them is to tease them. He would much rather be with "the boys." He is concerned about clothes, but only because he wants to be like the rest of the fellows. His pockets are crammed full of items he has collected. He is a little boy in nearly every way, and he will respond to you if you are interested in and understand the things little boys like. He won't even mind if you call him Bobby.

But before you know it, if you aren't alert, that boy will no longer be the same boy at all. You will call him by the same name, and he will respond. But he is different. How? You may see him sitting self-consciously by a girl. He probably isn't quite so boisterous while he has the attention of the girl. But listen to him if he is with other boys and wants to get a girl's attention! Clothes and appearance take on new meaning. He wants to look just right, at least for some occasions. His voice doesn't always do what he wants it to, and he is embarrassed by his mistakes. A new self-consciousness colors nearly every public action. He feels a compulsion to be just like everybody else.

You call him Bobby, and he answers; but he is not the boy you have known. He is becoming a new person, the product of a miracle which may go unnoticed by the unobservant. If you know your psychology at all, you know that Bobby is changing from a boy into a young man. He is no longer Bobby, but Bob or Robert. He is growing up. And woe to you if you continue to treat him as a child!

If the Sunday-school teacher makes no attempt to know his pupils and continues to teach Bob as he taught Bobby, no wonder so many young people who once attended Sunday school drop out between the ages of twelve and sixteen (four out of five). Repeated surveys revealing this sad truth are mute evidence of teacher carelessness or indifference, evidence that many teachers do not know their pupils.

This transitional period in the life of an adolescent may be more rapid and more noticeable, but there are similar changes in other age groups. The preschool child is in many ways unlike his older brother or sister in the Primary Department, just as Junior boys and girls are unlike the younger learners in the Bible school. Difference in age groups extends throughout the life span, with even younger adults differing in many ways from those in classes for older adults.

YOUR PUPILS ARE ALIKE

Your pupils have many general characteristics very much alike. Their needs are similar. Their levels of understanding are much the same. They respond to similar activities. Read through the characteristics below to find out what your age group is like. Although not exhaustive, this information will help you to understand your class.

CRIB BABIES—Birth to One Year

General Characteristics

Tiny, dependent upon adults to meet needs, cries to communicate needs, requires individual attention, sleeps a great deal, learns by the attitudes of those around him.

Needs

Loving physical care, clean surroundings, one worker for two or three children.

Level of Understanding

Absorbs attitudes of those who care for him, simple words.

TODDLER—Age One

General Characteristics

Constantly moving, learning to talk, learning through all five senses, limited vocabulary, imitative in action, attention span of no more than two minutes, requires individual attention, learning to be with other children, fearful, tires easily.

Needs

Frequent change of activities, frequent rest times, sense of security (own teacher, room, etc.), large-muscle activities, one teacher for three or four children, carefully kept environment.

Level of Understanding

Simple, brief stories using concepts of God, Jesus, Bible, and parents; retell stories often.

Activities

Conversation about pictures, simple stories, simple songs, action rhymes, simple puzzles.

TWOS AND THREES
Ages Two and Three

General Characteristics

Extremely active, attention span of three to five minutes, responds to guided play, rapidly growing vocabulary (although still limited), imitative in actions and speech, learns through all five senses, susceptible to disease, tires easily, achieving physiological stability, forming simple concepts of social reality, learning to distinguish right and wrong behavior, curious, learns by repetition, plays alongside others rather than with them, feels the love in a Christian atmosphere.

Needs

Frequent change of activities, stable environment, frequent rest periods, consistent discipline, sense of security (own teacher, room, etc.), large-muscle activities, repetition, one teacher for three to five children.

Level of Understanding

Simple stories, (retold often, using short sentences), appreciates Jesus as a friend and the Bible as a special book.

Activities

Guided conversation, guided play, fingerplays, simple songs, simple puzzles, simple stories.

BEGINNER—Ages Four and Five

General Characteristics

Very active, imitators, attention span of five to ten minutes, enjoys playing with other children, forming concepts of social and physical reality, inquisitive, learning to relate to adults rather than parents, big imagination, developing sense of right and wrong, learning to share, tires easily, growing vocabulary, curious, thinks of God in personal terms, responds to Jesus with simple trust.

Needs

Consistent discipline, stable environment, warm teachers who interact with him, frequent change of activities, consistent models of Christian behavior, explanation of new words, one teacher for five or six children.

Level of Understanding

Knows God created the world, loves Jesus and wants to please Him, thinks church is a happy, special place to go, willing to work with others, eager to help, shares, learns Bible words, invites others to come to Bible school.

Activities

Drama, guided conversation, guided play, fingerplays, music, puzzles, books, art activities, home living activities, block building.

PRIMARY—Grades One and Two

General Characteristics

Active, talkative, imaginative, likes group activities, asks questions, seeks personal attention from the teacher, small muscles developing, building attitudes toward himself, learning masculine or feminine role, learning to read and write, developing conscience and sense of morality, thinks concretely, honest, eager to learn, emotionally immature, attention span of seven to fifteen minutes.

Needs

Caring teacher, variety of activities, opportunities to talk, chance to display reading and writing skills, concrete stories and examples, security, patience, one teacher for six or seven children.

Level of Understanding

Appreciates the Bible as a special book, genuinely loves God and Jesus, prays sincerely, understands that Jesus is a special person, beginning to understand what sin is, can apply the Bible principles to everyday problems.

Activities

Dramatic play, storytelling, Bible games, art activities, music, puppets, reading.

MIDDLER—Grades Three and Four

General Characteristics

Energetic, healthy, thinks concretely, likes group activities, asks questions, enjoys personal attention from the teacher and other adults, continues to build attitudes toward himself, begins to demonstrate specific interests, "law and order" sense of morality, emotionally immature, eager to learn, memorizes easily, wants to help, attention span of ten to fifteen minutes.

Needs

Variety of activities for involvement in learning, caring teachers, opportunities to pursue and/or demonstrate interests, opportunities to help, concrete stories and examples, patience, one teacher for seven or eight children.

Level of Understanding

Chronology, application of Bible principles to life problems, Jesus as Savior, sin, need for salvation.

Activities

Projects, field trips, drama, role playing, puppets, Bible games, Bible research, art activities, music, reading, listening, memory work, using his own Bible.

JUNIOR—Grades Five and Six

General Characteristics

Energetic, healthy, loud, inquisitive, talkative, imaginative, wants to be like his peers, beginning to think abstractly, has many interests, likes competition, hero worshiper, dislikes outward display of affection, gang spirit, wants to be involved in classroom procedure, "law and order" morality, memorizes easily, activities affected by attitudes toward himself, developing attitudes toward social groups and institutions, independent, attention span of ten to twenty minutes.

Needs

Firm, loving discipline, involvement in learning activities, challenge to memorize, security in the midst of competition, encouragement, good examples of the Christian lifestyle, caring adults, one teacher for eight to ten children.

Level of Understanding

Chronology, what sin is, need for salvation, Jesus as Savior, Bible background, application of the Bible to daily problems.

Activities

Art, music, games, choral readings, memory work, Bible research, field trips, role playing, puppets, projects, using his own Bible, reading, listening.

YOUNG TEEN
Grades Seven, Eight, and Nine

General Characteristics

Awkward, growing rapidly, self-conscious, boisterous, independent, peer approval more important than adult approval, interested in the opposite sex, capable of abstract thinking, able to reason, developing his own faith and value system, definite interests and skills, increasing doubts.

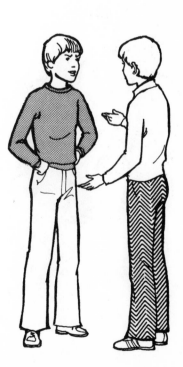

Needs

Guidance without pushiness, opportunity to make some choices of his own, consistent strong adult models of Christianity, warmth and acceptance by patient adults who are not easily shocked, challenging material, challenges and opportunities to serve, firm discipline, social activities in a Christian environment, one teacher for ten to twelve pupils.

Level of Understanding

Understanding and application of Biblical principles in life, what sin is, Jesus as Savior, interrelationships in Biblical material.

Activities

Field trips, Bible games, music, discussion, Bible research, role playing, problem solving, projects, using his own Bible, using Bible study tools, reading, listening, drama.

SENIOR HIGH
Grades Ten, Eleven, and Twelve

General Characteristics

Independent, rapidly increasing abilities, sometimes a "know-it-all," emotional, grown-up one day but a child the next, doubts, settling on his own value system and faith, physically mature, influenced by peer pressure, can reason well, interested in the opposite sex, thinks abstractly, choosing a vocation, cliquish.

Needs

Caring teachers who supervise without oversupervising, guidance, challenging material, challenges and opportunities to serve, social activities in a Christian environment, opportunities to express doubts and seek answers, vocational decision guidance, dating guidance.

Level of Understanding

Christian lifestyle; life application of Biblical principles; relationship of the Bible to science, history, and literature; worship; what sin is; Jesus as Savior; interrelationships in Biblical material.

Activities

Field trips, music, discussion, Bible research, role playing, problem solving, projects, using Bible study tools, reading, drama, listening.

YOUNG ADULT
Ages Eighteen to Twenty-four

General Characteristics

Selecting a mate or learning to live as a single, establishing a home, completing education and/or getting started in a vocation, settling into an adult faith, desiring a practical faith.

Needs

Practical Christianity applied to his life, opportunities to serve, people who care.

Level of Understanding

Finds the Bible a source of power; Jesus is Savior and Lord.

Activities

Bible research, art activities, drama, music, discussion, listening, service, personal study and prayer.

ADULT

General Characteristics

Who are these adults? Those in their twenties differ from those in their thirties who differ from those in their forties. Those in their forties differ from those in their fifties. Those in their sixties differ still, as do those who are older. So no two adults are alike, although some psychosocial adjustments must be made by all adults: rearing children, accepting the changes of aging, advancing in a vocation, adjusting to aging parents, handling emotions of both a positive and negative nature, establishing affiliations with one's age group, learning to accept death.

Needs

A personal, vibrant, growing faith.

Level of Understanding

The Bible as a guide; Jesus as Savior and Lord.

Activities

Bible research, art activities, drama, music, discussion, listening, service, personal study and prayer.

YOUR PUPILS ARE ALSO INDIVIDUALS

One basic truth must be repeated. It is this: each pupil is different. Each is an individual with God-given rights. Each is created and placed on this earth by God for the purpose of becoming a child of His. Never should a teacher merely teach a class. Always should the teacher teach the pupil. We often forget this divinely given standard of individuality. No matter who a person is, no matter how high or low he is in the scale of human esteem, he is God's creation. It is for him that God gave His Son. God loves that individual pupil with a love beyond human understanding and has entrusted his development to a teacher—to you.

As you review the characteristics of various age groups, keep this individuality of the pupil clearly in mind. Indeed, it may be rare for the teacher to find the characteristics of a single pupil in one particular section. The spread is even wider for a class group.

To study an individual pupil, read the characteristics with him in mind. What is the pupil's level of understanding? Has he progressed successfully through all of the earlier levels? Is he advancing logically and naturally toward higher levels?

To study a class, find the characteristics which coincide with the age grouping. Read the qualities of the age group above and/or below it. Note the spread of the group through several age groups. Learn what has been expected of the pupils and consider whether they have met those expectations. Note what is to be expected of them in the class beyond yours. Then study closely what the characteristics of your age group are and what is expected of them in the age level you are teaching.

Then, for further information, read and study training texts and other books which deal with pupils of the age you teach. The admonition is this: Teacher, know your pupil!

CHAPTER 4

KNOW YOUR SUBJECT

WHY DO WE STUDY THE BIBLE?

Little Betsy tugged at her mother's apron.

"Yes, Betsy, what is it?" Mother went right on drying the dishes.

"Mother," said Betsy, "why was I borned?"

Betsy's mother was a wise mother. She thought a minute, then said: "Why were you born? I'll tell you. God wanted a little girl like you, so He created you and gave you to Mother and Daddy to bring up as a child of His."

There in a nutshell is the plan of salvation, the purpose of creation, and the purpose of the home, of the church, and of the Bible. God, the Father, created every one of us in the hope that each will decide to be a child of His. We are free agents with the privilege of choice. All have sinned. Sin excludes us from God's presence, but He loves us so much that from the very beginning, back in the Garden of Eden, He inaugurated a plan whereby we can escape this penalty, be redeemed and restored as His children. The Bible is His revelation of that plan. That is its purpose.

It tells first of the creation, then of man's fall, then of God's plan through Abraham to bring His Son into the world to become its Savior. In Sunday school we study about Abraham and his descendants and their ups and downs. Then came the prophets who foretold the progress of the plan, including the coming of the Savior. At the time of God's choosing, the Savior came. He announced God's plan in detail, and it was heralded as the "good news" or the gospel.

God established His church for the dual purpose of telling all people everywhere about this plan and for helping them to be and to grow as children of God after they learn about it. He returned to Heaven, but left the Holy Spirit as a helper and guide to those who accept God's plan and strive to live by it. The Bible is described as the "sword," or the implement used by the Holy Spirit.

WHAT IS IN THE BIBLE?

In brief, the Bible tells how God's plan originated, how it developed, how it was put into effect by His Son, how we may avail ourselves of its benefits, and the reward in store for those who accept and remain faithful to it. It also tells of the punishment awaiting those who reject the plan. They will be cast into Hell, which is likened in the New Testament to Gehenna, the place for burning garbage.

This brief, easily understood explanation of why we have the Bible and what is in it has been the subject of more talk, more writing, and more study than any other subject in all the world.

WHY DO WE TEACH THE BIBLE?

You teach the Bible to enable your pupils to learn and to practice what God would have them learn and do. Earlier in this book we devoted a chapter to your purpose as a teacher. Here it is repeated in seventeen words—*to enable your pupils to learn and to practice what God would have them know and do.*

Books have been written about this purpose of yours. Some contend that you are to teach the Bible. Others argue that you are to teach the pupil. The soundest statement is that you teach the Bible to the pupil, helping the individual to learn what is in the Bible, what it means to him, and then leading him to do as the Bible says.

To accomplish this purpose you use the Bible as your textbook. You will gain help from other books and from your own experience, but the subject matter of the Sunday-school teacher is the Bible.

You will never know on this earth all that there is to know from the Bible. No man has ever known that much, and none will know during this lifetime. But you ought to know what the Bible is, how it came to us, how it is divided and, in a general way, what it teaches. Each Sunday's lesson then becomes a specific study, with our general knowledge as a background.

To obtain this general knowledge of the Bible you have much help. There are books about such subjects as "How We Got Our Bible." As has been stated, there are libraries of books about what is in it. You cannot read all of these books, but you can read some of them.

Perhaps your best help will be your own teaching. When you teach a lesson, you must study. This study will be of more help to you than it will be to your pupils. If you study each lesson as you should, and if you teach as you should, your accumulation of Biblical knowledge will be rapid.

That is one reason we shall not attempt in this book to give you an education in the Bible. The writers and editors of the lessons you teach will do more for you than anyone else.

But you need to take a training course, either alone or in a class, and attain proficiency in Biblical knowledge. There are many such courses. One of the oldest and best is called *Training for Service: A Survey of the Bible.* It is a revision of the book first published in 1907, which was a most important, if not the most important, book in developing the teacher training movement in the American Sunday school. It is a twenty-six lesson, elementary training book. In simplified fashion it sets forth what the teacher needs to know about the Bible.

But let the teacher know this:

1. He is never going to know everything the Bible has to teach, no matter how long he studies it.

2. The more he studies it, the more he will realize its depth of unattainable riches.

3. The more he teaches its contents to others, the more he will learn, for the teacher always learns more than the pupil.

4. Because he is a volunteer worker with many other duties, he does not have the time to do all of the preparation necessary. Therefore he is provided with quarterlies, commentaries, papers and other helps which aid him in his study of the Bible.

5. He ought, however, to understand the Bible to an extent that will help him to separate the wheat from the chaff in lesson helps.

6. He ought also to be better informed regarding the Scriptures than are those whom he is teaching. A wise man once told a young speaker who was to address a businessmen's club, "As long as you stick to your subject you are all right, for you know more about it than they do. Remember, in public speaking it is only necessary that you know more than your audience about the subject you are discussing. You do not need to know more than they about everything that is to be known."

7. The teacher ought to be aware of a great truth. The Bible is God speaking to us. Prayer is when we talk with Him, but in the Holy Scriptures God talks with us. Regard them accordingly. Never try to explain them away. Do not apologize for them. Do not put men's opinions ahead of them. Teach them for what they are—God's Word.

THE FIVE STEPS OF LESSON PREPARATION

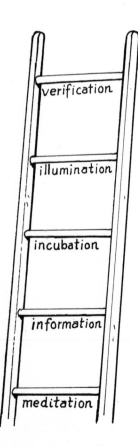

What has been said thus far in this chapter pertains to your general knowledge of your subject, the Bible. Now for a look at your weekly duty of studying the Bible in preparation for Sunday's lesson. This concerns your study of the Scripture, comments, and other available materials, as well as your own meditation and creative thinking.

This creative thinking is your part of the lesson preparation. It involves five steps, the five steps of lesson preparation.

The first step is meditation. To prepare your Bible lesson, find out, first of all, what God is teaching you in your life situation. Take the inward look before you seek to examine others.

The second of these may be termed information. To study your lesson you read the Scriptures, the comments the lesson writers have to make about the Scriptures, and perhaps you refer to other sources to complete your understanding of the lesson topic.

Then comes the period of incubation—brooding or reflecting upon the information you have obtained. You think it over, having in mind your class, each pupil in your class, and the needs of each pupil. You consider the methods for conveying the information to your pupils in the most effective way. You talk to God about the lesson and about your pupils, asking His help.

Then comes illumination. You catch the point. You see clearly what is to be done and how it is to be done. You become enthusiastic over the possibilities and are eager to "get the lesson into shape" for presentation.

The final step is verification, or revision. This is "getting the lesson into shape," making the outline. More will be said about this later.

HOW MUCH TIME SHOULD YOU GIVE TO LESSON PREPARATION?

Someone has said that it takes an hour of study for the teacher to get the lesson, two hours for the lesson to get the teacher, and at least three hours of study for the lesson to get the pupil. The true teacher, however, is constantly mindful of the lesson just ahead and is aware of the lesson to come. He is continually studying.

Here is how you do it:

1. At the beginning of a new quarter, consider the lesson course for the three months ahead. This course is part of a cycle of lessons, and you need to understand the general theme and arrangement of the cycle. The three-month course may be divided into units of one or more lessons. The term lesson, as used here, means something to be learned in a single Sunday morning class.

This Sunday's lesson is not a separate one, but is part of a unit. The thirteen lessons of the quarter usually have a general theme, divided into units. The fifty-two lessons of the year are part of a two-year, three-year, or six-year cycle of lessons.

2. Aware of the general lesson cycle, the three-month course, and the division of the course into units, consider next Sunday's lesson and its place in the quarter's arrangement of study. Begin by reading the complete Scripture text early in the week, perhaps on Sunday afternoon. In most lessons there is a complete text and a printed text. The complete text tells who is speaking, to whom, under what circumstances, and gives a general picture of the setting. The printed text includes the verses immediately pertaining to the lesson topic. The golden text or memory verse is a verse or part of a verse which pinpoints the central theme of the lesson. Read the complete text, read the printed text again, and meditate carefully upon the memory verse or golden text in this first reading. A wise suggestion is to read several versions or translations of the text in order to better understand it.

3. Then, early in the week, read the quarterlies, papers, and other commentaries available and mark them for further consideration. As you read, thoughts of particular significance for your class will come to mind. Note these in the margin of the page or in a notebook or on a paper pad for future reference. These thoughts may be suggestions for the lesson aim, how to open or how to close the lesson, or how to outline the entire presentation. All of this will be helpful when the time comes to plan the lesson.

4. Be on the alert for illustrative incidents. Your daily experiences, conversations with members of the class—almost any incident—may yield a nugget of thought to be added to the lesson's treasure chest.

5. Where do you study? Anywhere! At home, on the bus, during the lunch hour at work, at the public library, while waiting on the corner or in the doctor's or dentist's office. Those who do much studying, however, say that there ought to be a certain place, with ample time, for the fourth step of verification or revision, for "getting the lesson into shape."

6. In morning and evening prayer and talks with God throughout the day include an appeal for guidance in the lesson preparation. Experienced teachers testify that they have found this time of prayer the most profitable period for lesson preparation. In talking it over with God, they concentrate upon the truth He would have them emphasize and the method for making that truth a part of the lives of the pupils.

7. Some lesson courses include daily Bible reading which have to do with the week's theme. These readings are not all within the complete Scripture suggested for study, but they are related. Here, for example, in a quarter's study of the life of Christ as recorded in John's Gospel, could be a lesson, "The Good Shepherd." The complete lesson text may be the tenth chapter of John, the printed text John 10:1-11. The daily Bible readings recommended for that week may be as follows: Monday—"Faithful or False Shepherds," Zechariah 11:4-17; Tuesday—"The Shepherd's Parable," Luke 15:1-7; Wednesday—"The Good Shepherd's Voice," John 10:1-6; Thursday—"The Shepherd's Care," John 10:7-21; Friday—"False Shepherds Rebuked," Ezekiel 34:1-10; Saturday—"Feeding the Flock," Ezekiel 34:11-16; Sunday—"Our Faithful Creator," 1 Peter 4:12-19. Teachers who encourage their pupils to follow these daily readings are also blessed by having a class ready to understand and in a real way participate in the lesson.

8. Toward the end of the week set aside a period reserved for summarizing and perhaps planning the lesson. Thursday evening is a good time for this activity because it allows time for another session if needed. This early date also makes room for unavoidable interference such as illness or other emergencies. Earlier planning allows time also for the preparation of hand-work or for obtaining materials needed for the presentation.

In this final time of preparation, the lesson is planned, outlined, and made ready for presentation on Sunday morning.

In your study of the lesson, employ a habitual routine, but avoid the slavish rut of sameness. How can you expect the pupil to become mentally aroused if your own mentality is asleep? The church has too long been plagued by Sunday-school teachers who turn lazily to the pages of their favorite quarterly or other commentary and use it as a couch instead of a springboard in the preparation of the lesson. Their indifference is deadly. Teachers need a spiritual and mental revival once a week to keep them trim.

The quarterly, lesson paper, and other commentaries used by the teacher are necessary. Trained editors and writers give considerable attention to their preparation. But those editors and writers do not expect you to follow slavishly what they have provided. Their intent is to provide a body of material for you to divide, select, and refine in the furnace of your own thinking. The quarterly or other lesson commentary offers the ore in the rough. Your mind, attuned to the will of God and the needs of the pupils, melts out the silver and gold of truth for the individuals in the class.

Too much emphasis cannot be given to this need for careful, prayerful thinking on the part of the teacher. Here indeed is the secret of teaching. The teacher may be trained, have the very best of materials available, and plan lessons superbly. But unless he is stirred to the depths of his soul by the great truth of the lesson he is about to teach, he cannot possibly teach it as he should.

As you become more experienced, you will want to accumulate a personal library and use it in your lesson preparation. This library may grow until it contains many volumes. Among them will be a few which no successful teacher will want to be without:

1. Several copies of the Bible in various versions or translations. Each version has its merits and each has its objectionable features, but remember that no other writing in all of the world had even a fraction of the labor and care expended upon it as the Bible has had. We can trust its accurate transmission to us.

2. Bible dictionary to help identify and pronounce Bible words.

3. A Bible concordance. This is an alphabetical index of the principal words of the Bible with a reference and brief quotation for each occurrence. Suppose, for example, the teacher wants to quote Paul's famous "good resolution" as to his future, but can remember only the words, "I press toward the mark," or only the word "press" or the word "mark." He looks up the word in the Bible concordance and in a list of quotations in which the word is used. He finds the quotation is from Philippians 3:14. Or perhaps the lesson emphasis is upon faith or trust. He refers to the word in the Bible concordance and selects any number of quotations to which he wishes to refer.

4. Almost every Christian home has one or more hymnals to which a teacher can refer in selecting a hymn title or verse to use as a quotation. Some of the world's more beautiful poetry is found in hymns.

5. Usually the quarterly or the year's lesson commentary will be sufficient, but the growing teacher will have more and more use for a Bible commentary. Such commentaries are available in single volumes or multiple volumes.

6. An English grammar is "a must" since incorrect use of the language is unforgiveable. A modern dictionary is also useful.

7. As the teacher improves, he will accumulate a book of quotations, an encyclopedia, books of illustrative stories, and of course, books telling how to teach the particular age group with which he is working.

Again, however, warning is needed. Bookish lessons are not to be desired. The teacher's presentation must be enthusiastically alive, not academically dull. Study is basic in the teacher's preparation, but it ought not to come off as dullness in the presentation.

Do you want to be an enthusiastic teacher? Do you want to be so eager for the class period to come that you can hardly wait? Do you want to make the lesson period so interesting and so informative that your pupils will not want to miss a single lesson? Do you want to bring rejoicing in Heaven because of the good work you are doing? If so, the answer is found in thorough study, careful thinking, and prolonged prayer. There is no other way.

WANT TO CHECK YOUR STUDY HABITS?

	Seldom or Never	Some-times	Usually or Always
1. Do you set aside a certain time for study?			
2. Do you study other sources besides your Bible and quarterly?			
3. Do you make brief notes as you read?			
4. Do you classify this information in a way that will help your thinking?			
5. Do you look up new terms, learning pronunciation as well as meaning?			
6. Do you read carefully and slowly to get the meaning of what you read?			
7. Do you question comments which you read and try to learn whether they are based on facts or opinions before you accept them as true?			
8. Do you pray at least once a day about your lesson for the coming Sunday?			
9. Do you have a certain time when your lesson preparation must be completed?			
10. Do you check your method of study to see whether it can be improved?			

CHAPTER 5

KNOW HOW TO TEACH

WHAT IS TEACHING?

A teacher at the close of a summer camp seminar on teaching replied with one word to the question, "What do you propose to do first to improve the work of the Sunday school when you return home?" The reply was, "Resign." The teacher was joking, of course, but his joke had significance. Although it sounded as if he were discouraged, the truth of the matter is that his attitude held real promise. The teacher who realizes and confesses his inadequacy is prepared to improve. He has learned that teaching is difficult. Being a real Christian, he is challenged to make an important investment of time and effort in order to learn to teach.

What is teaching? Webster says that it is imparting knowledge or skill, giving instruction. Teaching in the Sunday school is more than the dictionary says. It applies to the heart, the soul, the life of the individual, as well as to the mind. The Sunday-school teacher is more than an instructor. He is a coach, a counselor, an adviser, as well as a pedagogue. Instructing the pupil in the knowledge of the Bible and coaching him in applying its principles to his life is a good description of the Sunday-school teacher's function.

YOU HAVE SOME EXCELLENT HELP

Don't be alarmed. This is not going to be a study of the science of educational psychology so much as it is an outline of some of the more practical rules of teaching. As in the two other requirements for successful teaching, knowledge of the pupil and knowledge of the subject, you have some excellent help for learning how to teach. This help is found in the quarterlies and other lesson helps. The writers and editors of these publications are specialists in teaching as well as in psychology and theology. Their services are at your command. In the lesson helps which they provide for your use, you will find every lesson presented in such a way that in studying it you also study the best way to teach it to your particular age group. All you need to know about teaching, therefore, is that it is important, that there are a few fundamental rules for success, and that you must follow these rules if you would succeed.

"Teachers are born, not made." Do you believe this to be true? It isn't. Good teachers achieve their success by study and hard work. True, some possess in a greater degree than others those traits which are desirable in a teacher, but this is only one small factor in success. You have native ability to teach. Everyone has. How successful you are depends upon the desire you have to develop your abilities to the maximum degree.

THIS IS THE KEY TO SUCCESS

"The desire to succeed" is the key to success. Our average teacher, you will recall, had no particular desire to succeed. He considered himself a success already, but he was mistaken. He could not possibly succeed without an eager desire to do so, and there was little evidence that he had such desire.

Teaching is a specialized function. It is more than merely handing out facts and information. It has been defined as helping the pupil to learn. Someone has said, "If the pupil does not learn, then you have not taught." Applied to the Sunday-school teacher, that statement is inadequate. It is incomplete. Of the Sunday-school teacher we must say, "If your pupil does not learn and does not live what he has learned, you have not taught." There is a vast difference in the two statements. It is not enough for your pupil to learn that God condemns stealing as a sin. You must help him build such a strong Christian character that he will refuse to steal. You must help him to determine that honesty in all things is to be a guiding principle in all of life.

Paul clarifies the teaching process in Colossians 1:9, 10 in which he points out the total teaching/learning experience. It begins with learning the facts ("be filled with the knowledge of his will"), proceeds to understanding the use and significance of those facts ("in all wisdom and spiritual understanding"), goes on to using that information in one's Christian walk ("that ye might walk worthy of the Lord unto all pleasing"), and completes the cycle with service ("being fruitful in every good work"). Teaching is incomplete unless it includes all of those elements.

You want to do this. As a sincere Christian, consecrated to the Lord's work, you want to coach your pupils in a way that will enable them to grow as Christians, to live strong, true, Christian lives. How do you do it? There are some rules to help.

NINE RULES OF TEACHING

Rule No. 1 is to know what is to be taught. When you go before your class, do you know exactly what you hope to accomplish during the lesson period? From a full mind (you have read extensively) and a clear understanding (you have meditated and prayed much until you have come to a clear understanding of what you intend to accomplish), you are now ready (you have carefully outlined your lesson and your purpose). This applies to all teachers whether of toddlers or adults. The teacher must know what is to be taught before he can teach.

Rule No. 2 is to know what changes you are seeking in your pupils' behavior. Do you want them to know some facts? That is a worthwhile goal. Perhaps you want to change an attitude. That is commendable. Even more significantly, you may want the pupil to respond with some change in behavior. That is essential. But you must decide before you begin why you are teaching this lesson. What do you want to accomplish?

Rule No. 3 is to gain and keep the attention of the pupil upon the lesson. Note the last three words, *upon the lesson.* To gain and keep the attention is not enough. This attention must be centered on the lesson, on what you hope to accomplish. How to gain attention and keep it centered on the lesson will be discussed in detail in a later chapter.

Rule No. 4 is to use words, terms, illustrations, and methods understood in the same way by pupil and teacher. The apostle Paul has some instruction for us in this regard when he says: "Except ye utter by the tongue words easy to be understood, how shall it be known what is spoken? for ye shall speak into the air" (1 Corinthians 14:9). Did you ever hear a teacher of Juniors using such words as "salvation," "consecration," "repentance," and other terms often used by preachers and teachers who do not explain what is meant? And how often do you hear a speaker use an illustration that is entirely unrelated to the experience and understanding of the audience? Note how Jesus used illustrations from material at hand: the sower, the flower in the field, the barren fig tree. The age level training books tell the teacher the understanding level of the age group. The lesson helps are written in words understood by the pupils of the age for which they are prepared. The same is true of illustrations. Those used are understandable by the pupils for whom they are written. A good suggestion here is that the teacher note carefully the words used by his pupils, then try to weed out of his teaching vocabulary any terms with which the pupils are not familiar.

Rule No. 5 is to lead the pupil from the known to the unknown. A good example of the use of this rule was when Jesus reappeared to His disciples (pupils or learners) after His resurrection. They had known Him, they remembered what He had said, and they had been horrified by His death. His resurrection had found them bewildered. Read Luke 24:44-48, and note verse 45: "Then opened he their understanding, that they might understand the Scriptures." Perhaps then you can understand why they who had been so fearful became at once so bold that they faced death unafraid. Such a change in the character of a pupil can come only when he is led by single, easy, and natural steps from what he says he knows to what the teacher wants him to learn. Learning to play the piano, a pupil first must distinguish the notes and by persistent practice learn to know and to play them correctly before he can undertake to translate a sheet of music into beautiful sound. The pupil in your class does not know the Bible as well as you know it. Your duty as a teacher is to know how far he has progressed in his knowledge and then to lead him from there into learning more. As his coach, or counselor, you learn how far he has progressed in his Christian life and after pointing out what he is to do next, to induce him to do it willingly with full understanding.

Rule No. 6 is to stimulate the pupil's own mind to action. This is easy when teaching children. Their eager minds are easily stimulated—they are almost too ready for action! But with older pupils it is different. Most people simply do not like to think. Thinking is hard work for them. Yet, unless they can be made to think, they will not learn. If they are stimulated to thought, if they participate mentally in the lesson, they find it much more interesting. Poor pupils in the Sunday-school classes of America! How often are they imposed upon by a poorly prepared teacher who drones through an uninteresting lesson. Poor Bible! How often it is made to appear dull and unappetizing because of a complacent and incompetent teacher. Poor Lord! He gave us a glorious message for all the world and a perfect method for taking that message to the world, only to see message and method made futile, of no consequence, because Rule No. 6 is not obeyed! If you do not stimulate the pupil to the point that he participates in the study and applies the teachings to his own life or his own situation, you have failed. Remember that.

Rule No. 7 is to actively involve the pupils in the learning process. A good rule of thumb is never to tell the pupils what they can find out for themselves in the time allotted. Choose appropriate learning activities which involve the pupils. A later chapter will introduce you to many of these activities and techniques.

Rule No. 8 is to require the pupil to reproduce in thought the lesson he is learning. Wait a minute! How can you require the pupil to reproduce the lesson in thought? In Rule No. 6 we learned that the successful teacher stimulates the pupil's own mind to action. In this rule, we learn that this action of the pupil's mind must be centered about the lesson. Have you ever listened to a sermon, then reviewed it in your mind to note how well you remembered it? This rule means that you are to teach the pupil so effectively that he can review the lesson afterward and tell what it means to him. He can do this, of course, only if Rule No. 6 is first obeyed, getting the pupil to think. But getting him to think is not enough. He must think about the lesson. He must be able to reproduce it in thought. In public school the teacher can tell whether he or she has obeyed Rule No. 8 by giving a test, requiring the pupils to reproduce what they have learned. In Sunday school such tests are sometimes attempted, but are not common. The teacher's cue lies in the interest shown by the pupil and any obvious progress in his knowledge and in his behavior. Read Chapter Eleven in this book which tells how to evaluate the pupil's progress in learning.

Rule No. 9 is to repeat, review, and otherwise reproduce the lesson, deepening its impression with new thought, linking it with added meanings, finding new applications, correcting any false views and completing the true. When a famous preacher spoke at a convention in Indiana one time, a Bible seminary sent its students to hear him. One of the students was heard to remark following the sermon, "He didn't say a single thing that was new." Told of the remark, the famous preacher said, "The boy was right. There is nothing new in what I said, for I preached a gospel sermon, and the gospel is two thousand years old. Nothing new has been added." That preacher's fame was not in preaching a new gospel, but in preaching the old gospel in such fashion that people gladly heard and believed. The same may be said of the Bible teacher. The Bible is not new. It tells us of God's plan for us, and that is all. In our teaching we must constantly review that plan, deepening with new thought the impression it makes upon the pupil. We must link it with added meaning to the pupil as he advances in his Christian living. This will help him correct false views he may encounter along the way, and establish his understanding of the true gospel. When this is accompished, the pupil will not only obey it fully in his own life, but will want to help carry out the Lord's assignment to all Christians; that is, to teach the gospel to everyone, everywhere in the world.

BUT RULES ARE NOT ENOUGH

These rules underlie and govern all successful teaching, whether in the home, Sunday school, public school, shop, office, on the farm—anywhere. They apply to the teaching of all subjects in all grades. You may be a successful teacher and have never heard of these rules. Not having heard of them, you do not consciously follow them. But reflect a moment, and you will discover that you use them. You must, if you are a successful teacher.

Still, do not be a slave to rules. You are to employ them, just as an automobile driver obeys the laws as he drives, but without thinking of the laws instead of his driving. Like the artist who masters the rules of perspective, balance, composition, color, the handling of his brushes and all the rest, and then uses them without thinking, keeping his mind all the time on the picture he is creating, you master the rules of teaching, then use them without being conscious of doing so. You can no more teach without following the rules than you can make a cake without using the ingredients required by the recipe.

YOUR BEST INSTRUCTOR

Your best instructor in teaching is your experience. As in all other achievement, we learn by doing. We learn to play the piano by practicing. We learn to drive an automobile by driving. We learn to make cakes by making cakes. We learn to paint a picture by painting. We learn to teach by teaching.

Particularly is this true for the Sunday-school teacher. Because, as has been explained, he has excellent guidance in the quarterlies or textbooks provided for his use. You as a teacher may take training courses in teaching—it is important that you do so. You may visit other classes in public schools and in Sunday schools to observe how other teachers teach—this is wonderfully worthwhile. You may read books on teaching—you should read one such book a year. At teachers' meetings you may give heed to the instruction on teaching and take part in discussions and demonstrations of teaching. All of these contribute to your mastery of the art of teaching—but, to repeat, experience is your best teacher. Your in-service training as a teacher will enable you to become better and better. But—and this final word is important—make sure that your progress is based on the nine rules of teaching outlined in this chapter.

INDICATORS OF GOOD TEACHING

Interest. When a pupil is interested, he will learn. An observant teacher will notice whether a pupil is paying attention. His facial expressions and behaviors will often reveal his level of attention.

Participation. Participation is an excellent way to learn, but the teacher must beware of the pupil who likes to participate merely to "show off." Watch for the quality and spirit of participation.

Attendance. A pupil who attends voluntarily because he is interested is usually learning. Absenteeism, on the other hand, is sometimes an indication that the pupil is not learning and does not consider the teaching worthwhile.

Activity. When a pupil does in daily life that which he is taught to do, the teacher is succeeding. If, for example, the lesson is about the Lord's Great

Commission and the pupil comes the next Sunday, bringing a visitor and explaining that he wants to carry out the Lord's orders, he demonstrates the teacher's effectiveness.

Flexibility. There is no one best way to teach. The effective teacher uses a variety of methods. When a teacher employs different methods, intended to meet different situations and to achieve different purposes, that is good teaching. The reverse is also true. When the pupil knows beforehand just what the teacher is going to say and do, when the teacher's methods never change, but are always the same, that is poor teaching.

Realism. Jesus is real, living, actual. His Spirit is with us. Ours is a living, all-powerful God. The Bible is His Word and not the semimythological record of a bygone day. The church is here and will continue forever. We are to live as children of the heavenly Father if we want to make a success of this life and the life hereafter. This is reality. Good teaching emphasizes this reality, denotes the emergency existing in every life, and appeals for an immediate verdict. Oh, for a way to banish the insipid, lackadaisical, semi-indifferent attitude of the teacher who does not measure up to the dramatic reality of the subject matter of the task!

Purpose. When the teaching is effective, both pupil and teacher know what they are doing and why.

Problem-solving. "That lesson helped me" is heard when the teaching is effective. A man in a Bible class said to the teacher, his eyes moist with tears, "Christmas means more to me this year than it ever meant before." Every pupil has problems. The Bible has the solution of those problems. Good teaching brings this solution to the attention of the pupil.

Behavior. The better the teacher teaches, the better the pupil knows God's will and the better he is led to observe it. When pupils discard evil habits, succeed in resisting temptation, make a practice of doing good to others, attend the church's services faithfully, the evidence is that the teaching is good.

If there is a behavior problem in your class—and what class doesn't have some such problems—the chart on the next page may help you.

HOW TO TEACH BETTER

If this is your pattern

1. The teacher talks. The pupil listens.

2. The teacher teaches with the quarterly in her hand.

3. The Bible text is all important. Let the pupil apply the teaching to his own life.

4. Voluntary pupil discussion is kept to a minimum because it takes too much time.

5. What the pupil says is not too important. He is present to learn, not to teach.

Move to this

1. The teacher leads. The pupil participates.

2. The quarterly is a tool; the teacher teaches from an outline, Bible in hand.

3. The teacher makes the Bible live by pointing out how its teachings are applied.

4. Pupil discussion is encouraged, but guided toward the lesson aim.

5. What the pupil thinks and says are important to him, and can help the teacher meet the pupil's needs.

6. "Covering the lesson" is paramount—and time is short.

7. Teaching is giving the facts. How this is done is unimportant.

8. I am teaching merely because no one else is available.

9. I lead a busy life and must sandwich my preparation into the spare moments of Saturday.

10. I'm a housewife. I'll never be able to master psychology, theology, pedagogy, and the art of teaching.

6. Achieving the aim is the goal—and eternity is at stake.

7. Variety in teaching gives zest to learning—and to teaching!

8. My Lord assigned my task. As His servant I shall do my best.

9. Teaching in the Sunday school is the most important thing I do. I'll do it well.

10. I'm a Christian. Like Paul, "I can do all things through Christ which strengtheneth me" (Philippians 4:13).

SUGGESTED CORRECTIVE ACTION FOR BEHAVIOR PROBLEMS

When the Pupil Acts Like This ➡ Here's What You Can Do

	Pray for Him	Give Lesson Assignment	Set a Good Example	Frequently Cite Good Examples	Offer a Reward for Good Achievement	Have a Personal Talk With Pupil	Give the Pupil Special Attention	Let Pupil Know What Is Expected of Him	Make Lessons More Interesting	Ask a Good Pupil to Be His "Buddy"	Investigate Background	Give Pupil More Responsibility	Introduce a Class Project
Attends Irregularly	X		X		X	X			X				
Fails to Pay Attention	X	X					X		X		X		X
Learns Slowly	X	X					X	X	X				X
Seems Overly Timid	X					X	X			X	X		
Likes to "Show Off"	X	X									X	X	
Appears to Be Antagonistic	X	X	X							X		X	
Tries to Domineer	X							X			X	X	
Is Always Tardy	X		X			X	X				X		
Lacks Reverence	X		X	X		X					X		
Does Not Attend Church Services	X		X	X	X	X			X		X		
Does Not Prepare Lesson	X	X	X		X					X			X
Brings No Offering	X		X						X				X
Seems Overly Aggressive	X			X							X	X	

CHAPTER 6

KNOW YOUR ROOM
AND EQUIPMENT

IS THE CLASSROOM IMPORTANT?

Addressing the Williams College alumni in New York, James A. Garfield, later to become President of the United States, said, "I am not willing that this discussion should close without mention of the value of a true teacher. Give me a log hut, with only a single bench, Mark Hopkins (president of Williams College) on one end and I on the other, and you may have all the buildings, apparatus and libraries without him."

True, the teacher is most important. Jesus, the Master Teacher, taught in homes, on the streets, in the field, on hillsides, in the temple, wherever He was at the time of the lesson. But none will deny that a classroom, well prepared and equipped, helps the pupil to learn, even when the teaching is superior. Indeed the classroom and equipment are among the important tools of teaching.

This importance must not be overemphasized, however. In many schools it is necessary to hold classes in nearby homes, under trees, in the church bus, theaters, public library buildings, firehouses, stores, and, in one case at least, in a barber shop. The use of such classrooms is an emergency measure, to be sure, the classes looking forward to the erection of adequate and proper facilities; but they are classrooms, nevertheless, and often the teacher does excellent work, refusing to yield to the handicap.

BRIEF CLASSROOM HISTORY

In the pioneer days of "the little red schoolhouse," the one-room church, with its Sunday-school classes divided only by benches or curtains, met the need. When it was realized that pupils learned better in groups, there came the demand for separate classrooms or alcoves. To meet this need, what was known as the Akron type of arrangement was developed in Akron, Ohio. This plan provided an auditorium surrounded by classrooms, or cubicles, opening into a main auditorium so that the entire school, each class in its own space, could participate in the opening assembly.

The next step was to graded assembly times with each department conducting its own meetings. This employed a variation of the Akron Plan arrangement with the classrooms or cubicles surrounding a departmental auditorium instead of the main auditorium.

Next came the educational unit plan in which the church modeled its school units after public school buildings. Each class had a room of its own.

More recent trends in Sunday-school facilities have emphasized larger department rooms, especially for younger age levels. At the same time, the department sizes are kept smaller than in the past. For example, a preschool department, limited to eighteen-twenty pupils, might meet in a room 25' x 25' with a variety of interest centers and movable partitions to allow for week-by-week flexibility. Carpeting and acoustical ceilings reduce the noise level to an acceptable volume. Similar arrangements for older age groups also permit easy movement from large groups to smaller groups and back again.

Newly erected church properties are often built according to a unit plan. A first unit provides for the Sunday-school classrooms and an auditorium for assemblies and for public worship. The second unit may provide additional classrooms or a worship auditorium. In the latter case, the first auditorium is then partitioned into classrooms. Additional units are provided as needed.

A current trend is to plan for multiple departmentalization for particular age groups in a large congregation. The key is for people of any age to find a relatively small unit in which they feel comfortable. There they can learn. A quick reference guide for suggested maximum department sizes is as follows:

Toddler (12 months to 2) 12-15
Twos and Threes (2's and 3's) 16-18
Beginner (4's and 5's) 18-20
Primary (Grades 1 and 2) 20-25
Middler (Grades 3 and 4) 25-30
Junior (Grades 5 and 6) 30-35
Young Teen (Grades 7-9) 40-45
Senior High (Grades 10-12) 45-50
Adult classes 30-35

Not every church has adequate facilities to make these kinds of department groupings, but this guide should provide a goal for future facilities.

Some churches compensate for lack of adequate space by planning dual Sunday school and worship services. Children may go to their classrooms for the full two hours or so for Sunday school and graded worship. Then youth and adults may have some classes conducted each hour, worshiping the other hour. A typical plan may work like this:

Hour 1—children's Sunday school, Young Teen Sunday school, some adult classes, a regular worship service.

Hour 2—children's worship services in their department areas, Senior High Sunday school, some adult classes, a regular worship service.

As a teacher, you are interested in this brief classroom history only as it pertains to your own situation. You have a classroom of some kind. Let us take a look at it and then at the equipment and teaching materials you use. Our part will be to mention the accepted educational standard, yours to compare your teaching facilities with that standard and see what improvements, if any, are needed.

A LOOK AT YOUR CLASSROOM

It should be clean. "Cleanliness is next to godliness" the old saying goes. A dingy, musty classroom, giving every evidence of indifference on the teacher's part, is inexcusable. Regardless of the place, the equipment, the carelessness of a caretaker, or any other circumstance, the room and its equipment can be kept clean. Juniors and older pupils will benefit by helping at a clean-up, paint-up party.

It should be attractive. Fresh curtains at the windows, the use of pleasant colors, a vase of flowers in season, Christian pictures or posters purposefully selected and properly hung, attractive bulletin boards—these and other devices are possible, even in less-than-desirable surroundings. The impression which the classroom makes upon every pupil teaches a lesson. A little child went home from Sunday school and asked, "Mother, is God poor?" Surprised, the mother replied, "Oh, no, God is not poor. He owns everything. Why do you ask?" "Well," said the child, "our Sunday school meets in God's house, and the chairs and things are old and broken. I just thought God must be poor to have something like that in His house." Pupils—adults and young people as well as children—are affected by the appearance of your classroom.

It should be educationally arranged. A rectangular room, with a ratio of three feet in length for each two feet in width, is most usable. The long dimension should be the outside wall. It is also best if there is at least one wall unbroken by doors or windows. The teacher stands with his back to a wall or a corner so that no light will distract a pupil or cause him discomfort.

It should be big enough to allow each pupil adequate space. This space varies with the age of the pupil. The active child of preschool age, unaccustomed to classroom confinement, requires the most space; adults require the least. Crowding interferes with learning. On the other hand, too much space per pupil is wasteful. A comfortable situation, with no crowding and with no lonely, discouraging chairs, is best.

It should be properly lighted. Glaring light is as objectionable as too little light. Curtains can be used to regulate the light from outside windows. A specialist from the electric company will advise you regarding the proper lighting levels. The lights should be placed so that no eye is offended.

It should be properly ventilated. Stuffy air makes sleepy minds. Too much fresh air, on the other hand, is uncomfortable. An electric fan blowing into the face of a pupil keeps him from learning, just as does a ray of sun shining upon him. If you want details, the public library has books telling exactly how many cubic feet of fresh air is needed per pupil per minute. But ordinary care and consideration will do in most cases.

It should be properly heated. In the cold months the room should be kept warm enough, and in the warm months cool enough, so that the pupil will be comfortable. This is not always possible, of course. Often, however, something can be done to help an undesirable situation.

It should be quiet. The use of sound resistant ceiling and wall materials will help. Storage cabinets and closets along dividing walls will deaden sound. Sometimes an active class of children can be assigned to a room where its activities will not detract. In one case the Beginners met on the first floor of the educational building and a class of women met in a room directly beneath. The tramping of the little feet as the children marched created a problem which was solved by the classes changing places.

It should be sacred. Such sacredness should be of two kinds: the room recognized and treated as a place set apart for the Lord's work and the class session protected from interruption. One class was found meeting in a room through which the pupils of an entire department had to pass. Dividing the one class into two, separated by a curtained aisle for those who had to pass through, was the solution to the problem.

HOW IS YOUR ROOM EQUIPPED?

As to seating? The furniture, like the lesson, should be graded to fit the pupil's needs. Each pupil's feet should be able to reach the floor. Educators know the exact height of chair desirable for each age group. The teacher's chair is in keeping with the pupil's. If the learner is a little person, seated near the floor, then the teacher also sits in a low chair, near the floor. If you teach preschoolers, consider the possibility of using area rugs and having the children sit on the floor for some parts of the Sunday-school hour.

As to tables? Tables, like chairs, are also graded to fit the pupil's needs. There are many kinds of tables of all heights. Some have adjustable legs which enable them to be raised or lowered as needed.

As to coat hangers? Coat hooks—and there should be coatracks or hooks available so that the pupil's wraps need not be draped over chairs or pews— likewise are graded. Little Miss Muffet, age five, hangs up her own coat on a coat hook suited to her height. Indeed, she may have an animal or flower to designate her chair and other equipment, or pasted on her coat hanger or hook. The coatracks may be separated furniture which can be moved from room to room if necessary.

As to supply cupboard? Almost every congregation has a carpenter who would enjoy making and mounting a neat, strong cabinet with ample space for storing handwork, papers, quarterlies, erasers, chalk, and other supplies used in teaching.

As to toilet facilities? In modern schools, these, also, are graded to the height of the pupils. The younger the pupil, the greater the need for readily available facilities.

As to chalkboard, bulletin board, flannelboard? Every classroom needs a permanently mounted chalkboard and bulletin board. These can be purchased, but skilled carpenters in your congregation could do it for considerably less cost. Flannelboards, portable or mounted, should be in all classrooms for children.

As to play equipment? In the Toddler, Twos and Threes, and Beginner Departments play equipment is needed, not for entertaining the child as a mere time-consuming activity, but with a definite teaching purpose in mind. Housekeeping equipment, blocks, and trucks are valuable assets for preschool learning. Such equipment should be sturdy, safe, and easily kept clean. Outside in the churchyard may be a grill, picnic tables and benches, shuffleboard courts and other facilities for older pupils, and teeter-totters, swings, jungle gym and slides for youngsters.

As to storage space? Storage space in storerooms and closets is necessary to avoid clutter, to provide for efficient learning, and to facilitate multiple use of rooms. It has been estimated that such storage space should equal one tenth the area of the rooms which they serve. One has only to glance into the average church storage room to realize how important it is that such space and contents be given attention to insure orderliness and proper care.

As to teaching materials? The Sunday-school teacher has numerous aids available for teaching God's Word: teacher's book, workbooks, handwork, activity kits, pictures, Bibles, maps, flannelgraph, filmstrips, movies, slides, songs, charts, tape recorders, overhead projectors, cutouts, books, commentaries—the list is increasing every day!

Much of this material is kept in the room's supply cabinet. The rest is kept in a common library, maintained by the church. The teacher borrows what is needed as it is needed. These materials are to be kept neatly, ready for use, and are to be checked frequently, to make certain that all is in readiness for the precious minutes of the class session.

YOUR PARTICULAR CLASSROOM

Facilities for classroom, furnishings, and teaching equipment have much in common for all grades. These have been discussed. In addition, each age level has its own requirements.

TODDLER

The *department* should contain no more than twelve or fifteen pupils, with thirty to thirty-five square feet per pupil. It should be on the ground floor near a rest room. The floor may be carpeted, but it must not contain a plastic fiber that scratches (like some indoor/outdoor carpeting).

The *furnishings* include low open shelves, slanted bookrack, small low tables, chairs with a seat eight inches from the floor (not folding chairs), a changing table and supplies, sturdy wooden doll bed, rocking boat/steps or indoor slide, an adult rocker, and a child's rocker.

Teaching materials might include books, wooden inlay puzzles, large cardboard blocks, a record player, baby dolls and blankets, and pull toys.

TWOS AND THREES

The *department* should contain no more than sixteen to eighteen pupils, with thirty to thirty-five square feet per pupil. It should be on the ground floor near a rest room; a southern exposure and many windows are very desirable. Carpeting helps to control noise but is not as easy to keep clean as a linoleum, asphalt, or vinyl tile.

The *furnishings* include chairs with seats ten inches from the floor and tables not higher than twenty inches from the floor. Pictures are placed at the eye level of the pupils. A low slanted bookrack displays books well, and low open shelves hold other toys and learning materials. A sturdy wooden doll bed, large enough for a three-year-old, and a wooden sink and stove make a realistic home living center.

In addition to curriculum supplies *teaching materials* should include books, simple wooden inlay puzzles, large cardboard blocks, record player, dolls and doll clothes, nature materials, play dough, large crayons, and an unbreakable offering container.

BEGINNER

The *department* should be on the ground floor, prepared for eighteen to twenty-two pupils and allowing thirty to thirty-five square feet per child. Clear glass windows, low enough for the pupil to see out, will add to their feeling of security. Carpeting or area rugs are good for noise control and for sitting on the floor for stories. Pictures should be placed at the eye level of the children. Add cheerful, homelike decorations.

The *furnishings* are to be low, round tables, ten inches from the seat of the chairs, low chairs with seats ten to twelve inches from floor, piano, record player, small table for flowers, and a wastebasket.

Teaching materials include pictures, handwork, activity books, blunt scissors, large crayons, clay, paper, paste or glue sticks, thick pencils, unbreakable offering container, and materials for learning centers.

PRIMARY

The *classroom* can be a section of a larger room, shut off by curtains or screens, although, of course, a more permanent classroom situation is desirable. Each classroom should have a chalkboard and other permanent fixtures outlined earlier in this chapter. The rooms should allow twenty-five square feet per pupil, with eight to ten pupils in each class.

The *furnishings* should include chairs twelve to fifteen inches high, a table ten inches above the seat of the chair, piano, pictures at the pupil's eye level, storage cabinet, and a wastebasket.

Teaching materials for the Primaries are many: workbooks, activity sets, handwork, Bibles, and such special things as construction paper, scissors, crayons, pencils, songbooks, and an offering container.

MIDDLER

The *classroom* should allow twenty-five square feet per pupil. Each classroom area should house eight to ten pupils. If several classes meet in a large room, movable dividers may be used to reduce noise and visibility.

Necessary *furnishings* are chairs, fifteen inches high; a table, ten inches above the seat of the chair; piano; pictures at the pupil's eye level; storage cabinet; and a wastebasket.

Teaching materials for Middlers include workbooks, Bibles, construction paper, felt markers, crayons, scissors, pencils, songbooks, an offering container, and maps and charts.

JUNIOR

The *classroom* should allow twenty-five square feet per pupil. Each classroom area should provide for eight to ten pupils. If several classes meet in a large room, movable dividers may be used.

Furnishings are less numerous than for the younger grades, but include chairs fifteen to sixteen inches high and a table ten inches above the seat of the chairs. Rubber-tipped chair legs will lessen noise. Pictures and bulletin boards must still be kept at the pupil's eye level.

Teaching materials are Bibles, workbooks, activity kits, pictures, handwork equipment, wastebasket, offering container, and relief maps of the areas being studied.

YOUNG TEEN

The *classroom* should provide twenty square feet per pupil for a maximum of ten to twelve pupils per classroom. If several Young Teen classes meet in a large area, reduce noise and visibility by using movable sound absorbing dividers or heavy curtains.

The *furnishings* can now be adult sized. Framed, permanent pictures and/or posters are desirable. The chalkboard is a permanent fixture.

Teaching materials include lesson leaflets, or workbooks, special kits, Bibles, maps, resource books, and posters.

SENIOR HIGH

The *classroom* should be planned for twelve to fifteen pupils, allowing eighteen to twenty square feet per pupil. Each classroom should be separated from other classes with dividers or walls.

The *furnishings* are table and chairs (now adult size), chalkboard, pictures or posters, wastebasket, and an offering container.

Teaching materials for the Senior High classroom are lesson leaflets or workbooks, Bibles, resource books, and maps.

ADULT

The *classroom* is to be individual, if possible, with a class of thirty to thirty-five pupils. Fifteen to eighteen square feet per pupil is considered adequate; under twelve square feet is poor.

The *furnishings* should be tables and chairs, although lapboards can be used by the pupils when rooms are crowded. Pictures are desirable.

Teaching materials include pupils' books, Bibles, resource books, paper and pencils, and maps.

Should you want to check further into fixtures and furnishings, you can obtain books listing a whole avalanche of items to be used in the Bible school or classroom. These books also include materials to be used and saved, time-saving suggestions for making equipment (with detailed drawings showing exactly how to make it) and hints for stencil cutting, mimeographing, and mailing. Indeed, almost any stationery store or public school purchasing agent can put you in touch with producers of all kinds of equipment. The church publishing house also catalogs equipment in addition to its imposing array of teaching materials.

Teaching materials for the Sunday school are becoming more durable, like textbooks, and can be kept for future use. The care and maintenance of them is the teacher's chore unless the church has a library for such materials. Usually, however, teaching aids and visuals are usable year after year.

TAKE AN INVENTORY

Now that we know about the classroom and equipment in general and about each age group in particular, suppose you take an inventory. Use the inventory form provided.

Class_____

Teacher_____

A. ROOM

Size: _____ feet by _____ feet

Number of pupils in class _____

Light: windows _____ size _____

        artificial _____

Heat: type _____ ; adequate? _____

Ventilation: summer _____

        winter _____

Good features:

Bad features:

Improvements needed:

B. EQUIPMENT

Tables: height _____; kind _____

Chairs: height _____; kind _____

Bulletin board, size _____

Chalkboard, size _____

Flannelboard, size _____

Supply cupboard _____

Wall pictures: (list) _____

_____

Visual aids: (list) _____

_____

Good features:

Bad features:

Improvements needed:

C. TEACHING MATERIALS (check ones used)

Quarterlies: teacher _____; pupil _____

Workbooks _____

Handwork _____

Pictures _____

Bibles _____

Maps _____

Visual aids _____

Good features:

Bad features:

Improvements needed:

Unit Two

Teach the Word of God

CHAPTER 7

FOLLOW A PLAN

EVERY MOMENT IS PRECIOUS

Having prepared yourself by knowing your pupils, by knowing your subject, by knowing how to teach, and by making certain that classroom and equipment are ready, you now come to the peak of your endeavor—you teach the Bible lesson. You have only a limited time at your disposal. Every moment is precious. Souls are at stake.

Successful lesson presentation depends a great deal upon preparation, but it also depends upon the plan you follow and the methods you employ. These are included, of course, in your preparation. But because they are so important in the teaching process, they are given an entire section.

This section includes a chapter on lesson planning and a discussion of the various parts of the lesson plan. Then will follow two chapters on methods—first, the methods of teaching by impression in which you, the teacher, do most of the talking, and second, the methods of teaching by expression, or participation on the part of the pupils. In your teaching, of course, you use both impressional and expressional methods; but first there must be a lesson plan, program, or outline. The final chapter in this section deals with classroom management, or discipline.

PLANNING THE LESSON

The universe operates according to orderly processes ordained by God. The earth on which we live is not the result of some accident or freak of nature. It exists and operates the way it does because God planned it that way. The Bible is a revelation of this plan and of God's plan for our salvation.

Man follows God's pattern. A pilot plans a navigational course. An architect plans a building before the builders begin to work. A homemaker plans a meal. Teaching a lesson, the Sunday-school teacher likewise follows a plan.

The plan which the teacher follows is important to the successful teaching of the lesson. First, consider the advantages of planning the lesson.

WHY PLAN THE LESSON?

1. By planning, the teacher can *determine the purpose of the lesson*. Just as the captain of a ship follows a charted course and arrives safely at a destination, the teacher follows a plan in an effort to accomplish the purpose of the lesson.

2. *Time is used effectively.* By following a step-by-step plan, the teacher does not waste the precious minutes of the class session.

3. *Unity, order, and continuity* enable the pupil to understand the lesson. These are achieved when the teacher makes a plan and follows it.

4. *A planned lesson helps the teacher to teach*. When the teacher goes before the class with a well-planned lesson, he teaches with confidence. He has control of the situation every minute, knows exactly what he is trying to accomplish and how he intends to do it. There is no "Now, let's see . . . what is next?" feeling about his teaching.

5. *Planned lessons are interesting lessons.* "The time passed all too quickly!" is the pupil's response to a planned lesson.

6. *A planned lesson is a half-taught lesson.* Because a lesson planned is a lesson half-taught, the teacher can give more time to making the teaching effective. He can do the planning at leisure and not by floundering from one point to another while trying to hold the attention of the class.

WHAT IS A LESSON PLAN?

A lesson plan is a step-by-step arrangement of the material and methods which a teacher intends to use in order to help his pupils to learn.

Through long experience and practice, educators know how learning takes place and the means by which it can be guided. As a result, we know that there are definite elements and processes present in every learning situation. Understanding these elements and processes, the teacher organizes them into an outline and uses this outline when teaching the lesson.

Because each lesson is different and because each class is different and each situation is different, it is necessary for the teacher to make a different plan for teaching each lesson. Each plan, however, employs the elements and processes of learning.

Also, because each teacher is different, the lesson plan is best when made by the person who is to use it. No stereotyped plan or outline is as effective as a plan made by the teacher himself.

WHAT IS THE CONTENT OF THE PLAN?

Following the basic principles of learning mentioned above and applying them to the Sunday-school lesson, an effective lesson plan should include the following:

1. *An objective, or aim.* This is a carefully thought-out, concise statement telling exactly what changes should occur in pupils' behavior as a result of this lesson. This is for the teacher's guidance.

The objective should be appropriate to the Bible content, to the age group, and to individuals within the class. You build a lesson objective by studying the Bible material, asking what is useful for your class. Then you determine what changes in behavior would result if this material were fully understood and applied. Write the objective in attainable terms.

2. *Materials*. These are the objects such as pictures, flannelgraph, handwork, music, or other materials that the teacher intends to use in presenting the lesson.

3. *A plan of presentation*. This is the lesson outline, written in detail, to aid the teacher to guide the pupils in the learning process. It includes information about the lesson subject and the methods and techniques to be used by the teacher in achieving the purpose of the lesson.

Larry Richards, in his book *Creative Bible Teaching,* suggests a four-step lesson outline.

—*Hook* gets the pupils' attention; bridges the gap between where the pupils are and what the Bible's message is for this class session.

—*Book* presents the Bible material; answers the question, "What does the Bible say?"

—*Look* explores ways in which the Bible material is useful in life. Answers the question, "What does this part of the Bible mean to me?"

—*Took* leads the pupil to commit himself to use the Bible material. Answers the question, "What will you do about this?"

4. *Evaluation*. This includes the methods, procedures, and devices by which the teacher measures the effectiveness of the lesson presentation.

These lesson plan parts overlap and are involved throughout the planning. The materials, for example, are selected to carry out the objective of the lesson and are included in the presentation. Evaluation, likewise, takes place throughout the whole lesson as the teacher decides whether the pupils understand what is being taught. However, all four must be included in the lesson plan.

THE PLAN IN OUTLINE

Lesson Title: _____

Quarter's Theme: _____

Unit Theme:_____

Scripture: _____

Objectives for This Lesson:_____

_____

_____

Materials: _____

_____

_____

Hook

How I plan to begin this lesson:

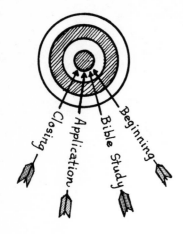

Book

Main Points in the Bible study:

    How these points
    will be presented

1.

2.

3.

4.

Look

Main Points of Application:

    How these points
    will be presented

1.

2.

3.

4.

Took

1. How I plan to get the pupils to commit themselves to action:

2. How I plan to close:

Evaluation

How I plan to evaluate the learning process:

Generally speaking, some such plan as this will guide the teacher in the lesson presentation. Now let us consider each section of this outline separately.

THE LESSON THEME

If you use a printed curriculum for your class, the lesson topic or subject is selected by a lesson committee and is carefully worded so that it sums up the teaching that the committee has in mind. The topic is chosen to appeal to the needs and interests of the age group and to keep within the background of knowledge achieved by pupils of that age. The topic is selected and worded for the pupils of a particular age group.

THE QUARTER'S THEME

In the Sunday school the lessons are arranged in three-month periods or a quarter of a year at a time. That is why Sunday-school textbooks are commonly referred to as "quarterlies." There is a different one for each quarter. Sometimes, however, the general theme extends for more than one quarter. For example, a study of one of the Gospels may cover two quarters.

THE UNIT THEME

The quarter's theme is usually divided into units. These units are sub-divisions of the quarter's theme, and the lesson is a subdivision of the unit. The lesson planners follow this arrangement so that the content is presented logically, under a unit theme, for better understanding by the teacher and the learner.

The teacher is to keep in mind the general theme, the unit theme, and the lesson topic, referring to them often and in a manner that will enable the learner to understand clearly the lesson subject for the day, its place in the unit under study, and the unit's place in the general theme. Unless the pupil has this understanding, each lesson is a disconnected study with no meaning other than the subject covered by the few short verses under consideration.

SCRIPTURE

The few verses in the so-called "printed text" of the lesson are not all that the teacher is expected to study. There is usually a background Scripture of which the printed text is only a part. For example, in a lesson, "The Resurrection and Our Faith," the printed text might be 1 Corinthians 15:2-8, 42-52, but the background Scripture would be all of 1 Corinthians 15. In addition, there are daily Bible readings selected by the lesson committee. These present passages from many parts of the Bible which will illuminate the topic for Sunday. By reading the background Scripture and following the daily readings, the teacher gains an understanding of Scriptural material bearing upon the Sunday topic.

The pupils may be encouraged to read the entire background Scripture and the recommended daily readings when preparing the lesson. They will find that such study will make the lesson more interesting and will enable them to learn more from the Sunday presentation. Even though the student does not read the entire recommended Scripture, it is essential that the teacher read it if he is to gain a thorough understanding of the topic text.

In presenting the lesson it usually is not possible to cover the background Scripture and other texts related to the topic. However, knowledge of them is necessary if the teacher is to develop the topic as part of the general theme.

THE TEACHING AIM

From the printed text (with full understanding of the background Scripture), the general theme, the unit theme, and the topic of the lesson, the teacher decides upon the lesson aim. The lesson discussion in the quarterly often suggests learning outcomes intended to appeal specifically to the age group being taught. The teacher may select one of these. Or knowing his particular group's interests, needs, and understanding of the Scriptures, he may decide upon a lesson aim altogether different from those suggested.

The lesson aim is the target, the goal, the purpose, the objective of the teacher's presentation. It is the lesson key, the thread on which the lesson is strung. It is the precise, exact, specific goal of the teacher's effort. An indefinite aim, not clearly thought out, is a bad aim because uncertainty in aim results in poor teaching.

An aim helps the teacher plan the lesson. Knowing where he is going, the teacher can plan how he is to get there.

An aim ties the parts of the lesson together. The opening is tied to the closing and links all parts in between.

The aim determines the teaching procedure. The opening and closing must be fitted to the aim. The emphasis upon the Bible's teaching and the application of that teaching depends upon the aim.

Evaluating progress during the lesson presentation and evaluating the effectiveness of the lesson after it is taught can be done only when there is an aim by which progress and effectiveness can be gauged.

Jesus had an aim. "The Son of man is come to seek and to save that which was lost" (Luke 19:10).

Paul had an aim, "I press toward the mark" (Philippians 3:14).

How to select the aim. Having read and carefully noted all of the material provided for the lesson, and keeping in mind the needs of your pupils (information), you pray for guidance and meditate at length (incubation) upon the lesson truths that may be taught. Keep in mind the theme of the quarter and of the unit as well as the lesson topic. Select several lesson truths you believe will help meet the needs of your pupils. Then combine them, or select the one best suited to the needs of your pupils, and thus arrive (illumination) at a single, condensed statement setting forth your lesson aim. Write it down. Check and recheck it, testing it to see whether it continues the lesson of the previous Sunday and looks forward to the lesson of the next Sunday. Make sure it utilizes the chief teaching of the lesson text and meets the needs of your pupils. Thus you arrive at the lesson aim, based squarely upon its foundation.

How to write the aim. Your aim should be carefully written out in a brief sentence. An effective aim should meet the following criteria.

A. *Clear.* It should communicate to the reader or hearer what you intend.

B. *Concise.* A good aim is stated as tersely as possible.

C. *Attainable.* An effective aim should be something which can be accomplished by this group in this class session.

D. *State in terms of pupil behavior,* the outcomes to be demonstrated at the end of the class session. A teaching aim is designed to bring about changes in the pupil. Therefore, it should be stated in terms of pupil behavior, not teacher behavior.

E. *Specific.* The aim should be stated in terms of specific, observable pupil behavior, something which can be measured for degree of achievement.

Consider these examples of teaching aims.

POOR: The pupil will learn the meaning of love in 1 Corinthians 13.

BETTER: The pupil will choose one way to demonstrate a quality of love to his family this week.

POOR: The pupil will discuss the way the church in Acts grew.

BETTER: From the book of Acts, the pupil will identify two activities of the early church which resulted in numerical growth.

POOR: To help the child to realize that Jesus is with us today.

BETTER: The child will name two ways in which Jesus is with him today.

Having arrived at a specific aim for the lesson, you are now ready to plan the lesson presentation from beginning to end.

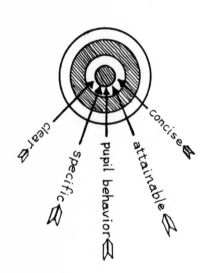

MATERIALS NEEDED FOR TEACHING

In preparing the lesson the teacher decides what materials will be used in the presentation. These include Bible and workbooks, flannelgraph, filmstrips or slides with projector and screen, pictures, pencils, paper, crayons, music, and any other items used to present the lesson.

BEGINNING THE LESSON

When a teacher takes his place before his class, the pupils are not thinking of the lesson. Their minds are wandering in as many directions as there are pupils. The Sunday morning experience of getting up, dressing, and coming to the church building as a family is not the ordinary, daily routine, and the pupil's attention may wander. The teacher's job is to catch the pupil's interest at the very beginning.

There is a formula for a successful lesson that the teacher ought to know. It is the same formula used by public speakers, by salesmen, by writers of advertisements and sales letters—by anyone who seeks to influence others. Here is the formula.

1. Catch the attention.
2. Hold the interest.
3. Create desire.
4. Inspire action.

In discussing the first of these, "catch the attention," or beginning the lesson, keep in mind these important points:

The opening should be brief. The Biblical content is to follow, and it is most important.

The opening should center attention on the lesson aim. A teacher could attract attention by mentioning news in which all were interested, but unless the news tied in with the lesson, the pupil would be confused, not helped.

The opening should be appropriate to the occasion. Firing a revolver into the air would attract attention, but it probably would not be appropriate.

The opening must not offend. "I am privileged today to be teaching a group of the best dressed, happiest looking, well-fed, prosperous, and contented group of robbers in town." This opening might attract attention and be true to the aim in a lesson on giving, but it probably would not be wise to use. A resentful pupil seldom learns.

Never apologize. "There are so many wonderful teachings in this lesson that we cannot possibly consider them all." This is a typical statement that does more harm than good. One teacher was actually heard to say, "Aunt Lucy was visiting me this week, and I just did not have enough time to prepare this lesson as I should."

Do not repeat. Variety is the spice of teaching. Do not use the same kind of opening week after week.

How many kinds of openings are there? Four classifications cover most methods for beginning the lesson.

1. *Calling for attention.* "Let me have your attention, please, and we shall begin the lesson." This may seem to be a natural and easy method for gaining attention, but a check of the suggestions for a successful opening will reveal its weaknesses.

2. *Using a focus for attention.* Before saying a word, the teacher unrolls a map and hangs it where all can see. Or he steps to the chalkboard and writes

a word or a sentence. One teacher arranged it so that when he stepped before the class to teach a lesson on the crucifixion, the lights were dimmed and a picture of Calvary was shown on the screen. Another, introducing a lesson on Christian growth, asked each person to take two pieces of chenille wire and shape them to show his growth. Teaching a lesson on faithfulness, another teacher introduced the person who had been a church member longer than anyone else and the pupil who had the longest unbroken attendance record. A teacher of boys, introducing a lesson on cleansing the temple, asked one student to display a whip he had made, similar to the one used by Jesus. Teaching this same lesson, the teacher of a women's class exhibited a mop, dust cloth, and similar articles and asked her class to name the activity with which they are associated—housecleaning. Holding up a collection plate, the teacher announced a lesson on giving. A teacher of preschool children held up a Bible and asked, "Do you know what this is?"

3. *Using an illustration.* "Once upon a time" catches the interest of everyone, even adults. "A sower went out to sow his seed," began the Master Teacher. There is no record of Jesus saying "Give me your attention, please." One of His chief opening devices was the parable.

The problem type of illustration for motivation is always a popular illustrative method. Beginning a lesson on the observance of the Lord's Day, a teacher of adults or children could say, "Do you like to go to the shopping center on Sunday afternoon? Let's make a list of the kinds of work people have to do in order to keep the stores in the shopping center open on Sunday. How do people neglect the observance of the Lord's Day because of this work? How could we show our interest in helping others have the opportunity to observe the Lord's Day?"

Another type of illustration could be the experience of a member of the class. "Have you ever been at a campground on a weekend and wondered what to do about worshiping on the Lord's Day? Could you have provided leadership for a worship service? What obstacles might need to be overcome? How successful do you think you might be? Have you been in a campground where someone has organized a worship service? Let's outline a suitable worship for the Lord's Day at a campground."

This method can be prepared in advance by asking a pupil to do preliminary research and bring a report, then calling for the report at the opening of the class.

News events can be used by a resourceful teacher, asking the pupils whether they have read the news, inviting one of them to tell of it, and discussing it. The others in the class may be asked for comments, leading into the lesson study.

Once alerted to the importance of an opening that will attract attention and focus interest upon the lesson aim, a teacher can discard a prepared method and seize upon another at a moment's notice, if it will be more effective.

4. *The question method.* Not the "How many have studied the lesson?" or "What is the lesson about?" type which puts the pupils on the defensive and does harm instead of good, but a catchy, interest-arousing question that leads directly into the lesson. Opening a lesson on Sunday observance, a teacher could ask, "Why do we come to the church on Sunday instead of Monday or any other day of the week?" Such a question could be adapted for any group as follows: Adults: "Why don't we work on Sunday just as on any other day?" Young adults: "What is your attitude toward Sunday observance? Should there be less or more restraint as compared to the present custom of observing Sunday?" Teenagers: "Why should Sunday be the best day of

the week?'' Juniors: "You aren't attending school today. Why?" Primaries: "Why do you like Sunday?" Preschoolers: "It's so nice for your Moms and Dads to bring you to the church building on Sunday!" One teacher, introducing a lesson on the cost of discipleship, said: "I am going to ask you a thought-provoking question: 'What is a man profited if he shall gain the whole world and lose his own soul?' " Bible questions can sometimes be used in this fashion. Another, introducing the same lesson, could be: "What question did Christ ask that demands an answer from every person in this class?"

Having attracted attention to the lesson aim, the teacher next holds the interest of the class by turning to the Bible.

MAIN POINTS IN THE BIBLE STUDY

"Let's see what the Bible has to say about it," ties the opening into the lesson. Since the Bible is the textbook, its teachings are vital. The pupil must understand what it says.

To help him to understand, the teacher pauses to review briefly what has gone before in the quarter's study, thus proceeding from the known to the unknown in the mind of the pupil. Perhaps a word about the lesson and the lessons to come will also help. Thus tying the lesson to what has gone before and what is to come is important. The lesson is not an isolated study. It is related to the others, to the unit and to the course as a whole. At the beginning of the Bible study is the usual time to make this tie-in with the other lessons. After this is done, the teacher is ready to consider the Bible text and the main points in the Bible study.

In considering the lesson passage, the teacher first makes plain who is speaking, to whom he is speaking, under what dispensation or Biblical era he is speaking, and for what purpose he is speaking. This may require explanation. It is necessary, however, if the pupil is to learn. Too often we confuse the pupil, and his interest in the lesson is lost when we assume that he knows that which he does not know. Even though he may be familiar with the facts to some extent, the repetition will tend to emphasize the importance of the lesson in his mind. The transition from our world of today to the times of the Bible is hard for the pupil to make. The teacher's task is to make the reading of the Scripture meaningful.

Help in understanding the Scripture passage is often available with a map, filmstrip, chart, flannelgraph, or chalkboard outline. The teacher's purpose in developing the Bible teachings is to make sure that they are thoroughly understood. Pupils are to be encouraged to ask about any passage which they do not understand.

As the teacher reads and explains or as the pupils read and explain the lesson text, the teacher keeps in mind (1) the general aim of the lesson and (2) the points he intends to make in the application of the lesson. He is going to refer to the Bible text in making the application and must make sure the pupil notes it, understands it, and remembers it.

The time spent in covering the printed Scripture text varies. In one type of lesson it may consume the major portion of the period. In another, where the text is already familiar to the pupils, the application may be given more time.

One way to emphasize the important Bible passages is to write them on the chalkboard. Another is to ask the pupils to underline them in their Bibles, workbooks, or lesson leaflets. This reminds us of the importance of every pupil having a copy of the lesson Scripture in his hands. When every pupil has a Bible, or lesson leaflet in his hand, he is more likely to be interested and therefore to learn.

Summarizing this discussion of the Bible background for the lesson, and how important it is, consider these three points:

1. *The Bible is the revelation of God's will.* The aim of every lesson is to lead the pupil to live according to God's will as revealed in the Bible.

2. *The Bible message needs to be known in terms of our present understanding.* The pupil is in the class because he wants to learn and understand the Bible. He is helped to do this by the Bible background or exposition of the lesson Scripture.

3. *The Bible has a message that is alive today and leads to eternity.* The lesson, therefore, must be applied to the pupil's daily living and his eternal hope.

THE LESSON APPLIED

"So what?"

The pupil does not ask the question this bluntly, but it is in his mind. "You have taught about Bible times and about an incident taken from those times, but what does this have to do with me?" If he is learning, he wants to know the answer to this question.

Here is the teacher's opportunity to apply the third principle of the formula. Having attracted the pupil's attention, then held his interest in what the Bible has to say, the third step is to create desire. The learner must be led to do what the Bible tells him is right. To create his desire to do it, the teacher must help him to relate the teachings to his own life.

Here, again, the teacher has the help of many methods discussed later in this book. Visual aids, questions, discussions, demonstrations, and many other interesting and convincing teaching devices are available.

Employing the demonstration method, one teacher, leading a group of adults in the study of a lesson centered about the text, "Except ye be converted, and become as little children, ye shall not enter into the kingdom of heaven" (Matthew 18:3) asked a little child who had been seated with his father to come to the front of the class. He took the child in his arms and introduced him. Then referring to the text, he explained that he was going to find out what a little child was like. He asked the child, "Where is your father? Can you point him out to us?" The child pointed to his father. The teacher, turning to the class, said, "Do you know God, your Father in Heaven? You pray to Him and you learn of Him, but do you know Him as this little child knows his father?"

Again, the teacher asked the boy, "I see you are smiling when you look at your father. Do you like him?" When the little boy nodded vigorously, the teacher said, "Here, put your arms around my neck and hug me and show us how much you like your father." The boy did so, whereupon the teacher said to the class, "Do you love God, your Father? If you do love Him, how do you show it? By being faithful to His teachings? By giving generously to His work? By serving Him? The great commandment is that we love God with all that we have. Are you like this little child in that you love Him without reservation?"

The little one was then asked whether his father fed him and clothed him and looked after him. The answers applied to the faith which we are to have in God. When, after several other questions, the teacher gave the boy a gift as a reward for his help, the little fellow took him somewhat by surprise with a loud, "Thank you!" The teacher, not to be caught off guard, instantly turned to the class: "Do you thank God for all that He gives you?"

74

Closing the demonstration, the teacher asked the boy whether he wanted to go to his father and whether he was sure that his father loved him and wanted him to come. With a shout of glee the youngster ran into his father's waiting arms. A pause, and then the application: "God wants you. He wants you so much that He gave His Son's life for you. Don't you want to come to Him—today?"

Pages in this book could be filled with similar applications of the great teachings of the Scripture. One of the best and most easily understood explanations, in chart form, is as follows:

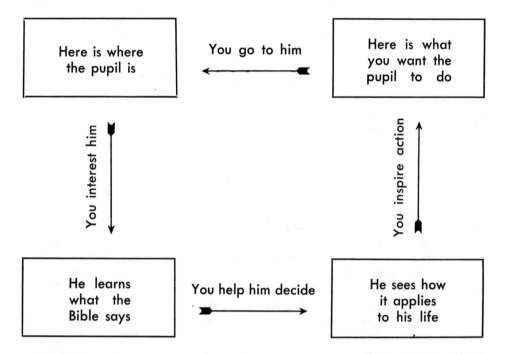

Note again how you must first catch his interest with the lesson opening and how you hold his interest by pointing out what the Bible has to say. (The reason that he is in Sunday school is because he wants to learn what the Bible has to say.) Third, you show him how the Bible teaching applies to his life. In other words, you create a desire on his part to live according to the Lord's will. Fourth, and finally, you inspire action on his part as you close the lesson.

CLOSING THE LESSON

Action is based upon knowledge plus decision and commitment to act. This element of action is present throughout the lesson, but comes to a climax in the closing moments which are all too often wasted amid the ringing of bells, checking of records, distribution of papers, and a hodgepodge of other activities. The devil must chuckle to note how the average Sunday-school lesson comes to a bedraggled finish.

Suppose that every time a salesman had the customer about ready to say, "I'll take it!" someone in the store would grab the customer by the arm and hurry him outside. If this were true, the store would go out of business. Yet, it is true of too many Sunday-school teachers. The jangle of the warning bell, a last-minute announcement, or some other disturbance seizes upon the pupil's interest and takes it away from the lesson just at the critical moment.

First, therefore, the teacher must arrange to have the closing moments of decision uninterrupted. By careful timing, he can conclude the lesson before the warning sounds.

In closing the lesson:

Remember the aim. The lesson objective has been kept before the pupil throughout the lesson presentation. It was brought to his attention in the opening. The Bible study was centered upon the aim. Again in the application of the lesson to the pupil's daily life, the aim was evident. Now, in the closing, the accomplishment of the aim is at stake.

Remember the pupil. Some of the pupils are not Christians, nor do they come from Christian homes where Christ is King. They must be led to accept Him as God's Son and to do what He has the authority to ask them to do. Other pupils either are Christians or are under Christian influence. They accept Christ as the Son of God. They must be helped to grow spiritually by doing His will. There are two parts, therefore, to every closing: (1) the call for recruits to Christ, and (2) the challenge to obey Him fully. These two parts are given in the Great Commission as recorded in Matthew 28:18-20: the teaching of recruitment and the teaching of conservation.

Methods of closing the lesson vary. Some lessons can be closed most effectively with a prayer, perhaps sentence prayers. An assignment, "Let's do something this week," is a good plan for some lessons, particularly when the pupils volunteer suggestions for action on their part. Sometimes an appropriate hymn can be read, played, or sung, leaving its message in the pupil's mind and the words on his lips as the lesson closes. "How many will do it?" with a show of hands, is recommended only when a decision is naturally arrived at, as in the case of bringing or inviting someone to Sunday school the next Sunday. Teachers have asked pupils to write a decision or resolution on a piece of paper and put it in their Bibles as a promise made to God. Pupils also have been asked to write a letter to themselves, sealing the envelope and giving it to the teacher who will return the envelopes to them for their own reading at a later date. Many devices can be employed, but this one point is clear: No teacher should ever conclude a lesson without giving the pupil a definite, personal objective, fully understood and appreciated as in keeping with God's will.

How Jesus closed His lessons can be a guide to the teacher. His so-called "Sermon on the Mount," which He "taught," was such a lesson, ending with the familiar houses built on rock and sand. In His famous lesson of "inasmuch" in Matthew 25, the parables of the sower, of the Good Samaritan, and of the prodigal son, His closing was an important part of the presentation.

Keep it to the point. The conclusion need not take much time. Brevity will give a suggestion of decisiveness. Be definite, direct, deeply concerned. Teach for a verdict. Teach for action!

LET THE BIBLE TEACH YOU

In reading the Bible, notice how the prophets, apostles, and particularly Jesus, the Master Teacher, began, applied, and closed their teaching. You will learn much from such Bible study. For example, note just a few instances from the teaching of Jesus as follows:

Beginning a lesson: Matthew 16:13-15; John 4:7.

Applying a lesson: Luke 24:19; Matthew 9:4, 5; 11:7-9; 12:11, 12; 18:17; 21:25.

Closing a lesson: Luke 9:20; John 21:15-17.

Take your Bible and read any of the notable teaching sessions related in the Scriptures. Note how the lesson was begun, developed, applied, and closed.

YOUR TEACHING PROBLEMS

The tardy pupil. Don't go back and review what has been said and done in order that a tardy pupil may learn. You have a closely planned presentation schedule and haven't the time. To do so is to reinforce his tardiness. Besides, the pupils who were thoughtful enough to be on time will lose interest. Greet the latecomer with a smile, but go right ahead.

The interruption. Interruptions are inevitable, although they can be reduced to a minimum. Do not be disturbed by them. One Sunday while a class was in session a storm was brewing. A brilliant flash of lightning was accompanied by an instantaneous blast of thunder which rattled the windows. Said the teacher, "God isn't ready for us yet. That one missed us!" Then he went right on with the lesson.

The arguer. Every class, even one of tiny tots, has its arguer. The wise teacher knows no one ever wins an argument, so she lets the arguer argue, occasionally taking some remark he has made and using it to amplify the point under discussion.

The ax-grinder. This is the person, usually in adult classes, who harps upon one subject all of the time. A smile and a "thank you," even though it interrupts him, usually leaves him mollified. Do not let him kill the lesson and the class with his harping.

Avoid favoritism. Some pupils are brighter and quicker than others. To avoid showing favoritism, make a deliberate effort to welcome comments from backward pupils and to involve them in any way possible. There will be opportunity enough to use the bright ones.

Discipline. Make the lesson so interesting in surroundings, so conducive to a respectful attitude, that lack of discipline is kept at a minimum. If a pupil continues to be a problem, try giving him a position of responsibility in the class. Visit his home and learn his background. Perhaps he receives too little attention at home and tries to make up for it in class. Or perhaps he is browbeaten at home and tries to make up for it in class by "getting even." Try praying for the troublesome pupil fifteen minutes each day, and you will find a solution.

Review your plan before class time. Few teachers are gifted with such phenomenal memories that they do not need to refresh their minds about what is to be taught and how it is to be taught. This review will make you master of the situation, eliminate unnecessary pauses in teaching, and keep class interest high.

But keep your plan flexible. Whether the pupil understands and decides rightly is the point. Your plan is not a law but a tool. When a better tool is presented, use it. A lesson should be planned flexibly enough so that variations in procedure can be made if necessary.

Complete the "Ten Checkpoints on Presentation" found on the next page.

TEN CHECKPOINTS ON PRESENTATION

☐ 1. Is everything in readiness in the classroom: the seats suitably located and necessary teaching aids on hand?

☐ 2. Is the method of presentation selected the one most suitable for the pupils and the particular objective of this lesson?

☐ 3. Does the lesson have a specific aim carefully selected?

☐ 4. Is the relationship of this aim to the unit and to the quarter's study clearly evident?

☐ 5. Does the presentation plan include some provision for getting the initial interest of the pupil?

☐ 6. Is the lesson built on the previous knowledge and understanding of the pupils?

☐ 7. Do the steps of presentation proceed from the known to the desired objective?

☐ 8. Has the relative difficulty of each teaching point been estimated?

☐ 9. Have the Bible teachings been definitely related to the daily life of each pupil?

☐ 10. In your plans for closing the lesson, are you sure that each pupil will be brought to make a definite decision and act upon it in daily life?

CHAPTER 8

USE METHODS OF IMPRESSION

METHODS OF TEACHING BY IMPRESSION

"What! Is the class period over already?"

"Boy! I'll never forget that lesson!"

"You'll like our class—it is so interesting!"

What teacher would not delight to hear such expressions from his pupils! When he does hear a pupil make this sort of comment, one thing is certain: he has used effective methods of teaching.

There are two ways in which an individual learns.

One is by *impression*—that is, he sees, hears, smells, feels, or tastes—uses the senses.

The other is by *expression*—he thinks, speaks, or acts.

Mostly, of course, the pupil learns by a combination of these two. But for the sake of simplicity, we shall consider methods of teaching in two categories:

Methods of impression in which the teacher attracts the attention, holds the interest, creates desire, and inspires action by using the senses, particularly those of seeing and hearing. This chapter will be devoted to a consideration of methods of impression.

Methods of expression in which the pupil learns by participating, by thinking, by speaking, or by doing. These methods of expression will be considered in the next chapter.

Jesus used both impression and expression methods as we shall see.

Effective use of any method of teaching must apply the three steps of instruction. These are: (1) *prepare* the lesson with an aim in mind, (2) *present* the lesson in a way that will achieve the aim, and (3) *evaluate* to decide whether the purpose has been achieved.

79

All learning starts with stimulation of one or more of the senses—sight, hearing, feeling, smell, and taste. It has been estimated that the total knowledge of a normal individual is gained as shown in the following graph.

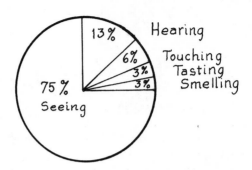

The Sunday-school teacher uses *visual methods* to show the pupil the truths of the Bible and how to apply them, *audio methods* to tell the pupil the teachings of the Bible and how to apply them, and to a limited extent, the *performance technique* to direct the pupil in doing what the Bible teaches him to do.

To be successful, a teacher must use all three methods. Telling is not enough. An instructor can tell the pupil how to drive an automobile, but the pupil does not know how to drive. Showing is not enough. The instructor can tell the pupil how to drive an automobile, then show him how to drive, but still the pupil is not entitled to a driver's license. Only when the pupil gets behind the wheel, starts the car, drives it, stops it, starts, drives, and stops it again and again until he does automatically all that is expected him, can he be accepted as a capable driver. We learn by being told, by being shown, and then by doing.

The first two steps are learning by impression. What we are to do and why we are to do it are impressed upon our understanding. The third step, that of doing, is learning by expression, or practice. An automobile driver improves with practice, as does a pianist, a golfer, a cook, a mechanic, or any other workman. The teacher's responsibility is to lead the pupil to study to show himself approved unto God, a workman that doesn't need to be ashamed. The pupil has to do the improving himself. The teacher cannot do it for him.

Now, let us consider in alphabetical order some of the more common methods of teaching by impression.

TIPS FOR USING AUDIOVISUALS

Any picture combined with words, such as a sound motion picture or a filmstrip or slides with accompanying recordings, is classified as an audiovisual. Prepared with voice, music, and other sound effects, this type of instruction carries conviction. Bible stories, illustrative experiences of individuals in home, church, or community life, pictures taken from nature with accompanying comments, or almost any other situation can be covered. Motion pictures, filmstrips, and overheads are the audiovisual projectors most often used.

The equipment is usually owned by the church and is requisitioned by the teacher from the library or other central source when its use is desired.

The first step, of course, in using any visual aid is to decide whether the aid will help to accomplish the teacher's purpose. The method is to conform to the lesson, not the lesson to the method. This is not always possible since the audiovisual message may not be exactly what the teacher needs. Previewing the presentation is a "must."

The second step must be to make certain that the method is superior to any other. If it isn't, then it is not to be used, regardless of how interesting or appealing it may be.

Make notes that will help you to complete the audiovisual message. It may include unusual scenes or situations, not familiar to the audience, requiring explanation. Questions may be raised which must be answered.

The pictured and recorded message is probably intended to lead to discussion. The discussion must be prepared for and be made to conform to the pictured and recorded pattern.

Explain to the group briefly what is to be seen and heard prior to the use of the audiovisual. You may also make listening assignments. Then make it clear why this particular message is being used. The group must be prepared if the method is to be effective.

BIBLE IN HAND

What It Is:

By "Bible in hand" is meant the Bible in the teacher's hand. The Sunday school is a Bible school. The Bible is the textbook, and the teacher should teach from it. Someone said that a man carrying a Bible as he walked down the street for a block preached a sermon a block long. The teacher with Bible in hand teaches the pupil to recognize, to respect, to believe, and to obey God's Word.

How to Use It:

Use the Bible to read from. The lesson text from the Bible is more effective than the lesson text recited from memory or read from a quarterly or lesson leaflet.

Use your Bible. Keep your outline in it, if you must. Keep the stories, questions, and other materials in it. But keep the Bible in hand as you teach.

Learn how to hold your Bible. Mark its paragraphs or lesson sections. Underline the words or terms for emphasis. A well-marked Bible is a well-used Bible. We don't worship God's Word. Rather, we worship Him and we use His Word to teach from.

Even when teaching Preschool children, the Bible in hand will be understood and will have its effect if the teacher says, "This is God's Book. God gave it to us. I'll tell you a story from it."

BULLETIN BOARD

What It Is:

A bulletin board is a board mounted to the wall which contains a display of materials related to the Bible lesson or the unit theme. A bulletin board is most effective when it presents simply a story, principle, or call to action.

How to Use It:

Plan a bulletin board carefully to carry out a particular theme, usually your lesson or unit theme. Use color and large figures and letters.

Change the bulletin board often.

CHALKBOARD

What It Is:

A teacher plus a chalkboard equal two teachers. A chalkboard is a smooth surface used for writing or drawing with chalk. The chalk may be of different colors. The board may be on the wall, as in a schoolroom, or it may be a smaller, movable size mounted on an easel or stood on a table or chair.

How to Use It:

It can be used for writing down points made in a lecture or discussion, answers to questions used during the presentation of the lesson, the lesson outline, or other writing prepared in advance of the class session.

Make the writing on the chalkboard large enough to be readable from any part of the room. Be sure that it can be seen from any part of the room as well. Use lower case letters when possible.

Often, a word or two, written during a lecture or discussion, will be adequate. Don't spend too much time writing, or you will lose the pupil's interest.

Learn to draw simple pictures outlining the lesson truth. Some teacher's books provide sample drawings. There are many books of simple drawings for illustrative purposes.

Keep the chalkboard clean and neat and in good repair. It should be pleasing to the eye. Always have on hand a fresh piece of chalk and clean eraser.

CHART

What It Is:

A chart or diagram is a technique which pictures information in some methodical form. It is a graphic method of teaching, particularly valuable because of its eye appeal. You will find one on page 95.

How to Use It:

Prepare charts in advance and have them ready to "flash" when you want them. Or you may want to have one exhibited in sight of the class before the lesson begins in order to attract attention and arouse interest.

Usually it is unwise to post a chart permanently. To cover the walls of a classroom with eye-catchers is to provide a distracting influence and put yourself under a handicap.

Use colors to indicate emphasis or variation in subject matter. Use the vivid colors and stay away from yellows (unless it is on black) and pastel shades.

The drawing should express the thought so clearly that only a few words of explanation are necessary.

One idea is to use a "strip chart"—strips of paper on a chart covering the outline. Remove a strip at a time as the lesson is taught point by point.

As in all graphics, be sure the chart is large enough and in a position to be seen by everyone.

Be careful not to stand in front of the chart when you talk about it.

Don't talk to the chart. Use a pointer and talk to the class.

DIORAMA

What It Is:

A diorama is a scene made in an open box. More elaborate ones may be prepared by adding small figures, grass, and objects.

How to Use It:

A teacher should make it in advance of the class session and use it during class.

Simple dioramas made in small boxes with pictures for the background may be used for handwork.

DISPLAY

What It Is:

A display is a collection of objects or pictures used to illustrate a principle or to present information. Display should include realistic materials.

How to Use It:

Displays are especially valuable for presenting information about Bible customs and mission fields. Set up the display ahead of class time. Then refer to it at the appropriate time in the lesson.

FILMSTRIPS AND SLIDES

What It Is:

Pictures in color for projection on a screen are available for nearly every scene and incident described in the Bible. The filmstrip is a strip of film containing a number of such pictures. A slide contains one picture. Most projectors can be equipped for the use of both filmstrips and slides.

How to Use It:

The equipment usually belongs to the Sunday school and is kept under the supervision of the librarian. Pupils can be trained to use it. When a teacher wants to use it, she should request it as far in advance as possible.

Make filmstrip and slide selections carefully, with a lesson aim in mind.

Preview the filmstrip or slides so that you will know the pictures so well that you do not have to study the screen while speaking to the class about the pictures. Many filmstrips have a narration on cassette or record, but you may want to give your own. Be sure to avoid lengthy discussions of the pictures.

Before the pictures are shown, explain why you are showing them.

Stand beside the screen and use a pointer to help in explaining a picture when necessary. Arrange to have the operator move each frame into position on signal from you.

Many filmstrips and series of slides tell a Bible story in chronological order, moving from incident to incident. Do not interrupt such a sequence unless necessary. However, assure the pupils that they may interrupt at any time with questions or comments.

If slides are used, arrange them ahead of time. Don't let the pupils catch you hunting for a slide. And be sure the slides are inserted correctly to appear right side up on the screen!

For more pupil participation, allow students to make their own slides. Assigned a certain Scripture verse or scene from the Bible story, each student can be responsible for one slide. (The picture from an old slide can be removed by soaking the slide in hot water. Be sure to remove slide from mount before soaking.) Use felt-tip markers to draw the pictures.

FLANNELGRAPH

What It Is:

Flannelgraph is a graphic method which uses adhesive backed pictures placed on a flannelboard in sequence as the story is being told or as the application of the lesson is being developed.

Because action is involved and the story or lecture is developed picture by picture, interest is kept at a high level. Also, because we learn mostly by what we see, the story or lesson is remembered. The flannelgraph can be used in all types of instruction for children. It is a vivid, therefore effective way to teach older students, too.

Because of its versatility and effectiveness it is widely used. The publishing houses which provide Sunday-school materials provide an increasing library of backgrounds and pictures for most Bible stories and most of the great teachings of the Bible. Books are available on how to make and use flannelgraph.

How to Use It:

Usually the flannelgraph equipment is owned and kept by the school under the supervision of a librarian and must be requested in advance if a teacher wants to use it. Increasingly, however, each teacher has the necessary equipment and applies to the librarian for story background and pictures.

The backgrounds are scenic and are fitted to the story such as an outdoor area, an interior house, temple-palace, or prison. Some stories require special backgrounds—for example, Daniel in the lions' den and the resurrection. Some need more than one background. Roll flannelgraph backgrounds on a cardboard roller to prevent wrinkling.

In presenting an object flannelgraph lesson, no background is needed. The pictured object is merely attached to the flannelboard.

Flannelgraph figures or objects come with a suede backing, several on a sheet, and sometimes must be cut out in advance. A manual is included in a packet to tell how to use the figures. Preserve the figures carefully so they can be used repeatedly.

As in all teaching, make the flannelgraph a means to an end, used only when it is the best method for that purpose.

Practice using the flannelgraph before actually teaching in order to make sure of just what you are to do and say. Keep the pictures in proper order, ready at hand, ready for use. The secret of success is the magical way of making a picture appear on the board with the touch of the hand. Put the picture on quickly, talking as you do.

Talk to the class, not to the flannelgraph. Be sure that every pupil can see and hear. Step aside after the picture is put on so that you do not hide it. Try having a pupil put on the pictures or objects as you talk.

Even though it is popular, do not overuse this method.

LECTURE

What It Is:

A lecture is an explanation. The pupil participates only as a listener. All teachers use it, even teachers of Preschool children. Usually, however, we think of it in terms of use with older classes, particularly adults. It is rarely used throughout the entire lesson, even when teaching a large class of adults; but is interspersed with questions, demonstrations, use of the chalkboard, map, or other object.

Christ often used the lecture method, usually before large groups. The so-called "Sermon on the Mount" was such a lesson. Even in that lesson, however, one can see Him pointing upward to say, "Behold the fowls of the air," or plucking a flower and holding it up for all to see, "Consider the lilies of the field." It was the content of His discourses rather than His manner and His method which the writers of the Gospels have preserved for us. He was so convincing in His presentation, however, that His listeners said, "Never man spake like this man."

How to Use It:

A lecture is used to explain the theme of a lesson, to connect it with what has gone before and is to come, to interpret difficult passages, and to present information not otherwise available to the group.

Make sure that it is the best method for your aim. Never be guilty of merely using the lecture method as an easy way to teach.

An effective lecture must be organized. When asked to what he attributed his success, a successful old-time preacher said, "I tell them what I'm going to tell them. Next I tell them. Then I tell them what I've told them. Finally I ask them if they understand."

Keep it short. Someone once said, "If you don't strike oil in ten minutes, stop boring." Interrupt your lecture now and then with a question, an illustration, or another device.

Be pleasing. Keep your pupils on your side as you talk.

Be sure that you are adequately prepared. Know what you are going to say and what points you are going to emphasize. Notes in your lesson outline will help you here.

Be sure that every pupil can see and hear.

Expect attention and get it. But be sure you deserve it.

Keep on the track. You have an aim. Hold to it.

Keep it simple. Use words your pupils can understand.

Speak slowly enough to be understood. A good rule is to talk only half as fast as you think you should.

But don't lose the attention of your pupils by going too slowly.

Be alert to pupil interest. If you detect lagging interest, change the tempo, use an illustration, mention someone's name, or employ some other device to regain attention.

Summarize at strategic intervals.

Cite examples. Make applications to the experiences of those in your class.

Evaluate as you go along. Ask, "Is that clear?" or "Does everyone understand?" or "Any questions?"

Keep it a Bible lesson. Refer to what the Bible says. If the pupils are Juniors or older, see that they have the lesson text in hand.

Keep the lecture clear. Concentrate on a few important points and make certain that they are understood.

Be human. A sense of humor, a smile, a "Let's talk this over together" attitude will help. Yet remember that you are in the Lord's house, in His presence, doing His work.

Keep the group in a problem-solving state of mind. Unless your listener is thinking, he is not learning.

Be considerate. Don't speak in a way a pupil cannot hear, nor so loudly that you disturb the class next to yours.

Be conscious of the time. Stop when time is up.

Speak to the individual pupil, for you are teaching individuals. Give each one the impression that you are speaking directly to him.

Avoid monotony. A monotone in speech, mannerisms repeated over and over, the use of the same words or terms or illustrations—these are fatal to interest.

Learn how to tell stories well.

Don't hesitate to be a bit dramatic now and then.

Be sincere. Don't say something if you don't mean it—and then practice it yourself.

The lecture has several advantages in Sunday-school teaching. These may be listed as follows:

1. Since pupils cannot be compelled to prepare their lessons in advance, and since few do except in those classes in which teachers employ methods which lead to lesson preparation, they are not prepared to participate. Pupils who discuss a lesson without preparation are doing no more than pooling their ignorance. The lecture method, therefore, while perhaps not ideal, is the only method available in many classes.

2. The lecturer or teacher, having a good understanding of the lesson and of the pupils, can impart information, appeal to the emotions and will of the pupils, guide them in their thinking, and inspire them in their daily living.

3. Time is limited in the usual Sunday-school class, and the lecture can cover more ground and make the best use of the few minutes available.

4. Not all classes can be seated in circles, squares, or other arrangements conducive to pupil participation. The lecture method is adaptable to classroom arrangement, can be used in a shortened or lengthened class period, and helps the teacher control the class under conditions which would prevent the successful use of another method.

5. Some classes, particularly of adults, are large. The lecture can be prepared and presented to a large group better than any other type of lesson.

6. It is easier to lecture than to teach by the discussion or question method. Since not all teachers are well trained in the more difficult ways of

teaching, and since many schools find it difficult to enlist and train enough teachers, the lecture is more popular.

7. In all Sunday-school teaching the teacher's personality is an important factor in the pupil's learning process. Usually the teacher has an attractive Christian character and leads the pupil in this way to become more like Jesus. Many who have forgotten the lessons remember the teacher.

The following suggestions may be helpful:

1. Attract the attention, hold the interest, create desire, and inspire action. As has been said, these are the consecutive steps of good salesmanship, and the teacher is a salesman. As a good example of these steps, read Acts 2:2-41.

2. Attention of the class to the lesson theme may be attracted in many ways. Care must be taken to avoid that which would distract rather than attract. One teacher, teaching a lesson on stewardship to a large class of men, began by taking out his billfold and extracting a crisp, new one dollar bill. He then asked the question, "Do you know the subject of the lesson today?" Again, when the Labor Day Sunday topic was "Growth Through Useful Work" and the weather was hot, he removed his coat, rolled up the sleeves of his shirt, and said: "The lesson this morning is about work." Since the Bible class session is not a formal session such as the worship service, unconventionality is helpful in centering attention upon the lesson topic. Care must be taken, however, to avoid overdoing the unusual, as it, too, becomes monotonous and therefore ineffective.

3. To hold the interest, the lecturer speaks directly to the class, adjusts his rate of speaking to the thought he is expressing, speaks distinctly and clearly so that all can understand easily, uses illustrations, facial expressions, and gestures in keeping with what he is saying. One successful lecturer deliberately plans what he calls "stepper-uppers" for use at intervals. These may be semihumorous illustrations, an object lesson, chalkboard or flannelgraph demonstration, a question, or other device. The teacher who began the lesson on stewardship by taking out a new dollar bill and putting it in an offering basket before him on the stand, used it later to recapture attention. He was making the point that God blesses the giver. Prior to the class session he had placed a greatly enlarged dollar bill in the basket. He mentioned the regular dollar bill he put in the basket, and then, to illustrate how God blesses the giver, he took out the much larger bill. One of the men mentioned months afterward that he had found by experience the principle that God blesses the giver is a true principle. He remembered and "lived" the lesson.

4. To create the pupil's desire to practice the Bible's teaching, the lecturer uses personal testimonials by Bible characters, great men of history, and other illustrations. He is careful to keep the lesson purpose clearly before the pupil so that the pupil knows exactly what his response should be. Persuasiveness is one of the finer arts of the lecture method and must be developed if the lecturer is to be successful. Teachers who use the lecture will do well to study the great speeches of history, make it a point to attend lectures, study sermons, radio and television appeals, and develop the convincing technique of good salesmanship.

5. After suggesting definitely what is to be done, the Sunday-school lecturer will encourage immediate action. Usually such a teacher concludes the

lesson with one suggested action for those who have not yet accepted Christ. In a lesson on giving, for example, the Christian pupils were encouraged to try tithing for a period, beginning that same day. Those who were not yet Christians were encouraged to do as the Macedonians who "first gave their own selves to the Lord." Sometimes the lecturer will suggest a specific project for the individual pupil or the class to undertake during the week. Always there is the specific suggestion of exactly what the pupil is to do.

6. Timing is vitally important to the successful lecture lesson. The teacher begins without hemming and hawing, follows a clear and easily remembered outline which he has planned carefully in advance, and drives carefully, without seeming to do so, toward a specific objective. He ends the lecture on time.

7. The lecturer uses notes to keep him on the track and on time. Sometimes the lesson outline is written on the chalkboard for the pupils to see as the lecture proceeds.

8. A pupil's listening vocabulary is smaller than his reading vocabulary. The successful teacher uses simple words and simple sentences.

9. The ear is slower than the eye. Therefore, the lecturer is careful to speak slowly and distinctly, to repeat for emphasis, and to sum up at intervals. Advertisers use repetition. Such slogans have helped make big industries. The method is not new. Jesus used it. His explanation of the kingdom of Heaven, Matthew 13:24-51, is a good example. When He had finished, He asked, "Have ye understood all these things? They say unto him, Yea, Lord."

10. The lecturer sets the tempo of the lesson, remembering that interest is lost when he speaks too slowly and is destroyed when he speaks too rapidly.

Summary:

To summarize what has been said on the subject, the following steps may be helpful:

Preparation step, to focus the attention of each pupil on the topic, immediately followed by an explanation telling what the lesson is to be about and why it is important.

Presentation step, to give the information, with key points easily understood, in logical sequence.

Application step, tying the lesson down with examples from experience to bring the thinking of the pupils into focus. This application step need not be delayed, but can be woven in as the lesson proceeds.

Testing step, with occasional pertinent questions, either to be answered audibly or mentally by way of check-up.

Summary of the key points, the conclusions, the crux of the lesson stated as simply as possible at strategic intervals and in conclusion.

Assignment, intended to inspire action as a result of this lesson and in preparation for the next.

MAP AND GLOBE

What It Is:

Maps are used in public schools in the early grades. They are always interesting. There are many kinds of Bible maps: the New Testament world, Palestine both in the Old Testament and the New Testament, the Roman Empire, missionary journeys of Paul, Assyria and adjacent lands as related to the captivities of the Jewish people, the kingdoms of Israel and Judah under the divided Hebrew kingdom, missionary map of the world with the prevailing religions of the world shown in colors, the exodus from Egypt, Palestine during the period of the judges, or Palestine during the ministry of Jesus. The variety is such that a special map of any era and of many events is available. There are also current world maps. Bible atlases of many kinds are also available.

Not only can these maps be purchased in various sizes with colors or to be colored, in three dimensions, or on flannelgraph paper, but a teacher or a class can make a map, learning in the process of doing so.

Globes are very useful for object lessons and missionary oriented talks.

How It Is Used:

Usually maps are kept in the library and loaned out to teachers upon request. Sometimes, however, when the quarter's lessons permit, one map can be used throughout the quarter and kept in the classroom. Such a map may be provided in the teacher's visual aids packet. In some classrooms a roller of maps is kept, allowing maps to be used as needed.

It is important that the map be large enough for all to see, that it is displayed where all can see, and that the teacher use a pointer to keep out of the way so that he talks to the class, not to the map.

A map can be used to capture attention at the opening of the class session or during the session.

A large map in sketchy form is easier to see than a small map in color.

Maps on slides, overhead transparencies, or filmstrips can be projected on a screen for study; they are also more easily seen in a large classroom.

Take care of maps. They can be used again and again.

OBJECT LESSON

What It Is:

Almost anything from an abacus to a zither can be used in an object lesson. Books of Bible object lessons are available, with talks fitted to almost any lesson aim. But the best object lessons are those devised by the teacher or by the teacher and the pupils. A classic object lesson is the use of a twig. It can show how easily a habit is broken when it is first started, compared with a heavier stick that has added strength and size as it has grown. Jesus used object lessons, such as setting a child in the midst as He taught: "Except ye be converted, and become as little children, ye shall not enter into the kingdom of heaven" (Matthew 18:3).

How to Use It:

Prepare in advance. Make sure that the object is at hand.

Impromptu reference to an object is sometimes effective. For example, a teacher may step to a window and say that the window must be clear and clean to let in the sunshine just as a Christian's life must be clean to let in the love of God.

In a lesson on faith or trust in God, the teacher of a men's class asked the men to take a coin from their pockets and look at the words, "In God We Trust," as he made his point.

Or the object can be displayed to arouse interest prior to its use, such as a kite, clearly displayed before the class from the beginning of the lesson, and used to illustrate the point that we must be held and guided by a stronger power than ourselves if we are to succeed.

Be sure that the object is clearly seen and understood by all before the point is made.

Sometimes a pupil can show the object and explain it. One teacher had a carpenter in his class demonstrate the use of the plumb line (Amos 7:7, 8).

After the object is used, unless there is some special reason for leaving it in view, remove it from sight so the pupils will not keep thinking of it and lose out on the development of the lesson.

Object lessons, like other ways of teaching, can be overused and become ineffective.

OVERHEAD PROJECTOR

What It Is:

An investment in an overhead projector can greatly benefit the teaching ministry of the church. The projector can be controlled from the front of a fully lighted room. A flick of the switch can divert the class' attention from the screen back to the leader. Brilliant colored images can be adapted to classes of any size.

Prepared transparencies can be purchased or found in some teachers' visual aids packets. Professional-looking transparencies can also be made inexpensively.

How to Use It:

Place projector at the front of the room. The head of the projector should be facing over your shoulder toward the screen. You should face the class.

Place a transparency on the projection stage and position it so that it will appear properly on the screen. Adjustments can be made by tilting the head of the projector or raising the elevating legs.

Adjust the size of the image by moving the projector toward or away from the screen. Focus the image by raising or lowering the projection head on its mounting bar by turning the knob.

Suggested uses for in-class learning activities:
—Trace places on a simple outline Bible map.
—Divide class into groups. Project assignments on screen that can be seen from all points of the room.
—Place a question or key word on the overhead to be viewed during pre-session time.
—Illustrate Bible narratives with simple stick figures.
—Project creative Bible projects for recognition and suggestions.
—Project cartoons to illustrate a lesson point.

Make your own transparencies:
—Create your design on paper.
—Trace the paper copy onto a transparency with a permanent ink marker.
—Add color for visual impact.

During a presentation, you may wish to cover parts of your transparency. This will aid in suspense and effectiveness as you control your classes' attention to the point at hand. The simplest type of cover is a piece of paper.

Store transparencies carefully in file folders or large envelopes for future use.

PEEP-BOX

What It Is:

Small pictures cut from Sunday-school cards or papers, or tiny objects made from wire, plastic and other material, can be used to construct a miniature scene at the far end of a shoe box. The scene is viewed through a small opening at the opposite end. Tissue paper of various colors and an electric light can be used to light the scene attractively.

How to Use It:

For small children use the peep-box for presession or to illustrate the scene of the lesson story. In older classes it can be a type of handwork.

PICTURE (FLAT)

What It Is:

A picture in hand or on a chart on the wall is among the oldest methods of helping a pupil learn by impression. Such pictures may be obtained for nearly every Bible story and for almost any other purpose as well. For example, a teacher of small children showed a picture of a happy child singing. "My, but this girl looks happy!" the teacher exclaimed. "What is she doing? Why of course, she is singing. I wonder what song makes her look so happy?" As the children then sing the song of their choice, they smile and reflect the expression of the child in the picture. Similar use is made of pictures in telling a Bible story. In older classes, pictures of scenes in the Bible lands or of objects, persons, or places pertinent to the lesson are helpful. Pictures can also be used to stimulate discussion.

How to Use It:

Select pictures suited to the age group—simple pictures with big figures for little children, more complicated pictures for older pupils.

Use care to get exactly the right picture or pictures that will help you to accomplish the lesson purpose.

Seek a picture with action and one large enough so that every pupil can see it when you use it.

Be careful to avoid unscriptural pictures or those which show a negative situation or action.

For Primaries, keep the composition simple, the content childlike, active, and vivid colors.

Middlers and Juniors will appreciate pictures which have more detail, are true to life, illustrate action and facial expression, and tell a story.

Older pupils will appreciate pictures with more symbolism and more detail. They also want better art.

Be sure the pupils, particuarly children, understand that the picture is only the artist's conception.

Take good care of pictures, for you can use them again and again. Mounted on cardboard and covered with clear self-adhesive paper (with record of its use on the back), a picture may be kept in a school file and used repeatedly by various classes.

Sometimes in a class of children the pupils can give a picture a title, or dramatize it, or tell what the picture says to them.

A picture can be used to review the lesson—"What did we say about this picture?"

PUPPETS

What It Is:

Puppets are personalities used to tell a story. They may be used to represent actual people. Or animals or objects may take on personalities to convey the information. Puppets may be made from paper bags, Styrofoam cups, construction paper, socks, clothespins, or a variety of other items.

How to Use It:

Children like to make their own puppets. This can be a type of handwork.

Puppets need to be realistic enough to be believable, large enough to be seen, and animated enough to be interesting. Use them to present or review information, to discipline, to teach songs, or to make applications. Books on how to make and use puppets are available.

READING

What It Is:

When the teacher motivates the pupil to read that which is said about the subject, he is employing one of the most effective methods of learning by impression.

How to Use It:

Individual pupils can be assigned specific reading and asked to report on it the following week.

All pupils can be enlisted to follow a daily Bible reading plan, the passages having been selected to apply to the next Sunday's lesson.

The six-way improvement plan encourages reading for lesson preparation. Using this plan, the pupil grades himself by checking six points on a card or an offering envelope bearing his name. The six points are his attendance, whether he was on time, brought his Bible, gave an offering, will stay for worship, and a particularly high percentage for having prepared his lesson.

In class, the pupils can be directed to study a verse or a passage to find a clue, a statement, or an answer to a question. Choral reading and reader's theater are practiced in many classes.

An adequate church library, with an alert librarian, can help the teacher to encourage reading.

Learn what is available in the public library on the subject, and recommend it to your pupils for reading.

RECORD PLAYER—TAPE RECORDER

What It Is:

A record or tape may be used to tell Bible stories, teach songs, relate actual incidents from mission fields or Bible lands, play back remarks or statements or songs by the pupils, and for many other purposes which require sound effect. Either can be combined with a visual medium to prepare multimedia programs.

How to Use It:

Be familiar with the record or tape being used. Review it carefully by playing it through several times.

Check the sound effects from all parts of the room to make certain it will be heard clearly.

Have it ready for instant use so that no delay will kill interest.

If another is to operate it, have him carefully coached in exactly what to do, when, and how.

As in the use of all other methods, make certain that it is the best for the purpose and that its use contributes directly to the lesson aim.

STORY OR ILLUSTRATION

What It Is:

Everybody loves a story—particularly children. It is a form of telling or relating an incident or experience as a means of accomplishing the lesson aim. Told properly, it makes the lesson come alive. It arouses the emotions. It directs the will.

Jesus made use of the story method. More than fifty of His stories are recorded. About half of them are short, like the brief comparison, "A city that is set on a hill cannot be hid." The others are longer, like the parables of the good Samaritan and the prodigal son.

The good teacher will master the art of storytelling. Teachers of older pupils also use it to illustrate.

How to Use It:

Remember that storytelling is a teaching tool, a method. Use it as a means to an end. Make it help to accomplish the aim of your lesson.

Tell it; don't read it.

Keep the story the right length: Toddler, two to three minutes; Twos and Threes, three to five minutes; Beginners, five to seven minutes; Primaries, eight to ten minutes; Middlers and Juniors, ten to twelve minutes.

Remember to use words familiar to the listener.

Grade the appeal to the age group: Toddler and Twos and Threes—action, fingerplays, gestures; Beginners—stories of babies, parents, brothers, sisters, home, Sunday school, play; Primaries—stories which incorporate action and color; Middlers and Juniors—Bible hero stories, missionary, adventure; Young Teens—stories of challenge and adventure.

Make the story positive, constructive, containing the highest ideals.

Use mostly Bible stories.

Make sure that the pupil knows what is fanciful and what is real.

Beware of overusing the story method. Be sure that it is the best method for the purpose before you use it.

Keep the lesson aim clearly in the mind of the listener.

Study storytelling. There are excellent books available at the bookstore or the public library. Or you can borrow some from your public schoolteacher friends. Or have the church librarian order books from the publishing house.

Open a story in a way that will attract attention. "A certain man had a fig tree . . . ," "A certain man made a great supper," "There was a certain rich man which had a steward," "There was a certain rich man which was clothed in purple and fine linen," "Two men went up into the temple to pray." Note how Jesus began His stories.

Picture the events of the story as scenes and the characters as real people. Make it live!

Put yourself into storytelling. It is showmanship of the highest order. Utilize voice inflection, facial expressions, and gestures. Choose your words such as "sleepy, slow, still," or "quick, hurry, fast, run, busy, awake, alive!"

Build to a climax: the princess sees the baby Moses, the three Hebrew children walk out of the fiery furnace, the prodigal son comes home—these are climactic situations.

Close the story properly. A good story teaches through the experiences of its characters. You don't have to go back over it and point out the applications. A brief, summarizing statement, tied to the aim, the objective, the purpose of the story, is all you need. Note how Jesus ended His stories.

Prepare carefully so that you will not leave out a vital incident. Have in mind the story's outline. A good way to do it is to keep in mind the sequence of incidents or of characters. For example, a good way to recall Bible history is to relate the characters: Adam, Noah, Abraham, Moses, and on to John at Patmos.

Use dialogue, changing the voice, facing about for each character, picturing one as tall and another as short by raising or lowering the hand, and using other devices that will come naturally to the good storyteller.

Make the story convincing. You look afar off, down the road, to see the prodigal son approaching.

Review the telling of the story in your own mind after the lesson is finished. Write down the good points and the bad points to help you to tell the next story better.

OTHER TEACHING AIDS

Other teaching aids enabling the pupil to learn by impression are numerous. Stand-up, cut-out figures depicting the lesson; mural; model; viewmaster; movie projector; split/35 strips; the sand table or box—the resourcefulness of the teacher and publishing houses provides an ever increasing variety of such helps.

METHODS OF IMPRESSION

What are the methods of impression in which the teacher does everything and appeals to the senses of the pupil? Here is a chart listing such methods and indicating the degree of effectiveness for each age group:

The Method	CRIB BABIES Birth to age one	TODDLER Age 1 to 2	TWOS AND THREES Ages 2 and 3	BEGINNER Ages 4 and 5	PRIMARY Grades 1 and 2	MIDDLER Grades 3 and 4	JUNIOR Grades 5 and 6	YOUNG TEEN Grades 7-9	SENIOR HIGH Grades 10-12	YOUNG ADULT Ages 18-24	ADULT Ages 25 and above
Hearing: Lecture						3	3	3	2	2	1
Record Player	1	1	1	1	2						
Story and Illustration		1	1	1		2	2	3	3	3	3
Seeing: Bible in Hand	1	1	1	1	1	1	1	1	1	1	1
Chalkboard					2	1	1	1	1	1	1
Chart						3	3	2	1	1	1
Diorama				1	1	2	2				
Display				2	2	1	1	2	2	3	3
Filmstrips and Slides				3	1	1	1	1	1	1	1
Flannelgraph			1	1	1	1	1	1	1	1	1
Map and Globe					3	1	1	1	1	1	1
Object Lesson				3	2	1	1	1	1	1	1
Overhead Projector						2	2	2	2	1	1
Peep-Box			1	1	2	3	3				
Picture	1	1	1	1	2	3	3				
Puppet	2	2	1	1	1	1	1				
Reading					2	1	1	1	1	1	1

1 Important 3 Can Be Used

2 Useful ☐ Not Used

Which of the methods of teaching by impression do you use often? Occasionally? Which should you use more often than you do now? Which are not appropriate for your use? Following is a simple checklist for answering these questions.

MY METHODS OF TEACHING BY IMPRESSION

	I Use Often	I Use These Occasionally	I Should Use More	Inappropriate for My Use
Bible in Hand				
Bulletin Board				
Chalkboard				
Chart				
Diorama				
Display				
Filmstrips and Slides				
Flannelgraph				
Lecture				
Map and Globe				
Object Lesson				
Overhead Projector				
Peep-Box				
Picture				
Puppets				
Reading				
Record Player, Tape Recorder				
Story or Illustration				
Others: _____				
_____				
_____				
_____				
_____				

CHAPTER 9

USE METHODS OF EXPRESSION

METHODS OF GAINING PUPIL PARTICIPATION

When we learn to drive an automobile, play the piano, or make a cake, we may hear someone tell us how it is done, or we may read how it is to be done. We may even see someone else do it, but we still do not know how to drive an automobile, play the piano, or make a cake. We must do it ourselves. The more we do it, the better we do it. Practice makes perfect. This is known as learning by doing, or by participation, or as educators say it, learning by impression plus expression.

Remember, when someone tells us or shows us, we are learning by impression. When we do it, we learn by expression. Both methods are necessary.

Applied to teaching in the Sunday school, the expression method means that the teacher must gain the participation of the pupil. In the pupil's mind, consciously or unconsciously, is the principle of "Use me or lose me."

Use me or lose me.

Jesus demonstrated the fact that expression is an essential factor in learning. His method was "Hear, then do." Note His appeal to the disciple, or learner: "Arise," "Come," "Follow," "Go," "Make disciples," "Tell," "Walk," "Watch," "Work." It is impossible to become a Christian without actively practicing or participating.

The teacher leads the pupil to learn by getting him to participate in the class session and then to practice in daily life the principles learned in the Bible class. The pupil learns by participating in the learning process. When he does not participate, he does not learn.

Whether the aim of the lesson is for an understanding of the Bible or the application of Bible truth to life, the pupil must participate actively and know that it is for a purpose. The pupil's activity may be easily observed such as participation in an action rhyme for the very small child, asking or answering questions for older children, and discussion in older groups. Or the activity may be largely mental such as thinking through a proposition presented by the teacher, solving a problem, or arriving at a general conclusion.

In any class, old or young, no two pupils are alike. A class is much like a fruit tree—some pupils are ripe and ready to understand what is being taught, some are nearly ripe while others are half ripe, others are partly green, and some are entirely green. The teacher cannot plan for the advanced pupil or for the entirely green pupil, but he must plan to engage the participation of everyone. This may be accomplished by different means for different age groups. The teacher will learn which methods are most effective after he studies the pupils and after he has tried several methods.

The purpose of pupil participation is the teacher's constant aim—to get the pupil to think. Merely to give the pupil something to do to occupy the time is a sinful waste of opportunity. Keeping the little hands or the big minds busy is not enough. The "busy-ness" must be for a purpose. It must contribute to the attainment of the lesson aim. For example, putting the children in a Primary class to work coloring pictures is worthwhile pupil participation only if the activity helps to accomplish a definite lesson purpose. Engaging the minds of an adult class by means of an interesting illustration is wasted time unless the illustration bears directly on the purpose of the lesson and will be effective in accomplishing that purpose.

When a pupil reproduces in his own mind the truth being taught, he is learning. He is not learning until he participates in this manner.

Merely pouring out knowledge is not teaching. The teacher who talks on and on, telling what he knows without arousing mental response, is wasting his time and the pupil's time. He is getting nowhere.

Nor is true learning mere memorization and repetition of the words of the teacher, of a quarterly, or, for that matter, of the Bible. Catechism may have its merits as a method of imparting truth. For children, particularly those in the elementary grades, memorization is recommended. But catechism alone is not education. It is memorization.

A pupil is sometimes said to have learned the lesson when he has committed it to memory and can repeat or recite it word for word. Education would be simple if this were true. It is not true, however; when the pupil is merely reciting, he is not participating at his most productive level.

The teacher's aim is to teach the pupil not only the words, but the thought of Scripture. In teaching the Bible, it is important to know and to remember words, but it is even more important to know and to remember the lesson thought.

The pupil is to be encouraged to express the lesson truth in his own words. Sometimes the thought will be expressed crudely. The capable teacher will pardon the pupil's inability to express the thought acceptably while he encourages the pupil to think more accurately in order to express himself more adequately.

As the pupil advances in participation, he will give a reason for that which he believes. He will discover a truth, seek proof for that which he has discovered, voice these proofs, and thus become a stronger believer than the one who believes but does not know why or who cannot explain why. The Bible teaches that we are to find out for ourselves if these truths are so. Even the youngest pupil will take a stronger hold of the truth if he can see a reason for it. In searching for proof, the pupil also encounters new knowledge on the way, just like the mountain climber who finds the landscape always widening around him. The teacher's effort to encourage the pupil to seek out proof for a truth that is taught is made effective when the learner participates by telling of the proof which he has discovered.

The participating pupil's next advancement is found in the study of the application of knowledge. Having his mind stirred by the presentation of a truth, then seeking and discovering verification of that truth, he next applies the truth to his own life. The boy who finds a use for what he has learned in his lesson becomes doubly interested and successful in his schoolwork. What was idle knowledge now becomes practical wisdom. The learning process is completed when this stage is reached.

This progressive participation varies, of course, with age. The mental activity of younger children lies close to the senses. Their ability to think is limited. As they advance in age and in the learning process, they begin to think. Next, they begin to apply to their own lives that which they have been thinking.

Summing up this process of participation, the teacher is to:

1. Help the pupil to understand clearly the lesson aim.

2. Get him to express in his own words (or in his own thoughts) the meaning of the lesson as he understands it.

3. Aim to make the pupil an investigator, finding for himself whether a certain statement is true, and thereby being able to give a reason for his opinions. Until he learns the truth for himself, he does not know it.

4. Motivate the pupil to apply to his own personal life and circumstances the truth which he has heard, investigated, and proven.

Not only does participation help the pupil to learn, but it also makes the class session more interesting and vital, both to teacher and pupil. Every teacher can remember the class session in which the dismissal bell seemed to come too suddenly. Where did the time go? Everyone was so busily occupied that the time just flew. Each was so keyed up throughout the session that he was almost sitting on the edge of his seat listening and participating. But every teacher can also remember the class session which, it seemed, would never end. The pupils were restless, indifferent, and unappreciative. Illustrations fell flat. Nothing seemed to arouse interest. The class session was a dismal failure.

What made the first so interesting and the second so dull? Why was the first class so absorbing and the other so boring that both pupils and teacher thought it would never end? The answer may be given in two words—pupil participation. In the first class, the pupils were so interested that they were thinking. In the second class, the pupils' interest was not sufficiently aroused to make them think. When a pupil does not take part, he does not think. When he does not think, he does not learn. The teacher's task is to make him learn. To do this he must make the pupil think. To make him think he must lead him to take part.

How does the teacher get the pupil to participate? To repeat, the methods vary for the different age groups. The successful teacher learns which methods are most effective for his age group by study, by observation, by trial and error. He then employs those methods, singly, in combination, and with adaptations to meet the situation.

The Sunday-school teacher cannot compel participation as can the teacher in the public school. But the public schoolteacher, if asked, will admit that compulsion is the least effective method.

Nor can the Sunday-school teacher reward the pupil for participation as the public schoolteacher does when she administers grades. But, again, the public schoolteacher knows that the pupil who participates merely to gain a good grade is not learning as well as he should.

Only when the pupil's interest is engaged to the point that he willingly participates because he wants to is the learning process most effective. It is in this highest realm of interest that the Sunday-school teacher must function. His task is to so engage the pupil's interest that the pupil will voluntarily, of his own free will and because of his personal desire, take part as a learner.

How is the pupil led to take part? Repeating again, the methods for each age group are different. But every method for a particular group will not succeed in every class for that age level. The teacher must discover which methods are effective, and use them. That is an important part of the teacher's function.

The careful teacher also will consider obstacles which interfere with pupil interest. What teacher has not attracted the attention of the pupils and rejoiced at getting the lesson off to a good start, only to have the learning situation marred by some unavoidable influence. It may be worthwhile to discuss a few of these obstacles.

1. *Disturbing noises* are all too common in the Sunday school. Not all noise can be eliminated, but much of it can by discussing the problem at the Sunday-school teachers' and officers' meeting, by a discreet use of signs and announcements, by a proper example on the part of the teachers, by installation of carpets, and by use of soundproof ceilings. Often mere recognition of the problem is the most important step toward its solution.

2. *Interruptions* by secretaries, treasurers, superintendents, or others are unnecessary except in case of dire emergency.

3. *Self-consciousness on the part of the pupil* must be taken into consideration. Often an informal, friendly attitude of the teacher will result in a more comfortable feeling by the pupil. Seating the pupils around a table or in a circle may help avoid stiff formality.

4. *Physical discomfort* interferes with interest. Overcrowding, poor arrangement of classroom, inadequate light, poor ventilation, or an unattractive classroom will make class interest difficult. Too hot, too cold, bare floors, bare walls, dingy curtains, broken chairs—these are indicative of neglect and are found in the Sunday school far too often.

Now let us consider nineteen ways (arranged alphabetically) by which you may enlist pupil participation in the lesson. An explanation of each and suggestions for using the method are included.

ASSIGNMENT

What It Is:

The assignment method consists of the teacher asking a pupil to prepare in advance for participation in the lesson. The method is best for teenagers and adults, but can be used in classes of Middlers and Juniors.

How to Use It:

Plan assignments well in advance.

Make sure that the pupil's effort will contribute to the achievement of the lesson aim.

Arouse interest before the assignment is made. The teacher may say, "Next Sunday we will study about giving money for the Lord's work. What questions would you like to have answered about giving?" With encouragement, such questions as "Who is to give?" "How much?" "When?" and "Why?" are asked. The teacher makes assignments, asking pupils to find the answers and to be prepared to give them in class next Sunday. To help the pupil, the teacher can write the question on a piece of paper, listing Scripture verses for the pupil to read in order to find the answer.

Keep the assignments within the range of the pupil's previous knowledge. Pupils given the questions on stewardship, for example, must be able to know how to read, how to find passages in the Bible, and that giving is expected of the Christian.

Define carefully just what is to be done, making certain that the pupil knows what is expected of him.

Avoid embarrassing a pupil by insisting that he accept an assignment. He may have a good reason for not accepting. As a safeguard, it is wise to have a pupil in mind when the assignment is planned, perhaps even talking with the pupil about it beforehand.

Do not make the assignment too difficult or too simple.

See that the pupil who accepts the assignment goes through with it. Telephone to ask how he is progressing. Stop and see him with a suggestion or two.

Many types of assignments are possible, including definitions of Scriptural words, finding an answer to a question, bringing objects or pictures or other information, doing something such as making a call or writing a letter, interviewing someone, gathering data, taking a poll, or conducting an experiment.

Be sure to call for a report on assignments.

Show sincere appreciation for completion of assignments.

BUZZ SESSION

What It Is:

A buzz group is a small group of three to seven people who buzz (talk) for a brief time about a problem assigned to them by the teacher. They arrive at a group conclusion which is then presented to the class as a whole. This is useful with youth and adults.

How to Use It:

Usually a buzz group is assigned to discuss some aspect of a general subject. For example, if the subject is stewardship, one group could make a list of needs for money in the local church work while others could list needs in other fields such as home missions, foreign missions, benevolences, colleges, and other work to which the congregation contributes.

Each pupil should know exactly what is expected of him.

A time limit of not more than ten minutes is set and strictly observed.

Be sure to allow time for each group to make its report.

Express appreciation for the work done.

Keep the subjects directed toward the lesson aim.

Let each group select its own chairman who will keep the discussion on the subject and see that everyone participates.

Let each group select its own reporter who will relate the summary of the group's findings.

CHECK CHART

What It Is:

A check chart is a questionnaire which may be answered by checking the answers to questions. One appears on page 130.

How to Use It:

Prepare it in advance. It needs to be typed and reproduced so that each pupil may have one. If it is necessary, it could be written on the chalkboard for the group to work on as a whole.

Keep the questions directed toward the purpose of the lesson and within the ability range of the pupils.

Explain carefully what the pupils are to do and why.

Make sure that each pupil has a pencil if the check chart is for individual use. Each person will also need something to write on.

Keep the answers confidential unless pupils are told otherwise ahead of time.

COLLAGE OR MONTAGE

What It Is:

A montage is a series of pictures arranged in order to expand a theme. The pictures usually overlap each other so that no white space is left. A collage adds a three-dimensional effect to the pictures.

How to Use It:

Pupils may make collages or montages to illustrate applications of Bible material. Provide necessary materials to complete it.

Plan enough time for pupils to make the project and then to explain it.

This is a useful method for Beginners and older.

CONVERSATION

What It Is:

The teacher and the pupils talk about the lesson theme in a conversational manner, not as a discussion.

How to Use It:

Conversation is used frequently for teaching children. The conversation usually occurs around a browsing table or in an interest center.

The teacher leads in the conversation, often using a question to establish contact. For example, the teacher may say, "What do you have in your hand, Charlie?"

From some such simple opening, the teacher proceeds to direct the talk in a way that contributes to the achievement of the lesson aim.

Carefully avoid preaching or lecturing, but do try to get the pupil to become so interested that he will talk with you about the subject.

DEBATE

What It Is:

Two teams participate—the affirmative and the negative. Each debater speaks briefly. After all have spoken, one member on each side has a few minutes for rebuttal to disprove the other team's claims and to reaffirm his own.

How to Use It:

Pupils can be assigned to teams in advance in order to do research work and other preparation.

Do not take all of the class period for the debate, but allow time for a brief explanation at the opening and for comment by the other pupils at the close.

The debate method is most appropriate for teens and adults.

DISCUSSION

What It Is:

Discussion is one of the most effective means of getting pupil participation. It may be used in classes with older children up through adults. One of its chief advantages is discovering and clarifying misconceptions. Discussion is also an effective way of determining just what each pupil needs to know to complete his understanding of a subject. It also encourages pupils to think.

How to Use It:

Discussion comes most easily when the group is seated around a table or in a circle with the teacher sitting in as part of the group.

Encourage every pupil to participate. When he does, let him know that his comments are welcome. That can be done with a smile, a nod, or a word of encouragement.

The purpose of the discussion must be made clear to all, particularly to the teacher. Everything which is said must contribute to the achievement of the purpose.

Good discussion procedure follows these six steps: (1) objectives or aims are clarified, (2) problems are analyzed, (3) facts are assembled and studied, (4) pros and cons are considered, (5) advantages and disadvantages are discussed, and (6) efforts are made to arrive at a conclusion.

Avoid arguments. Suggest reference to the source if the argument is about factual information. If the difference is in the field of opinion or interpretation, make the fact clear and invite the class to give consideration to both points of view.

DRAMA

What It Is:

Drama may range from pantomiming a Bible story in a children's class to writing and producing a dramatization to apply a Biblical truth in an older class. In either case, the pupil learns by acting out a part.

How to Use It:

As in every other situation in teaching, keep the dramatization true to the lesson aim.

Bible stories are the chief materials for this use, although missionary stories, historical episodes, lives of noble men and women of past and present, and problem situations with their solution as taught in the lesson are all source materials.

Keep the presentation within the understanding and interest level of the participant. Children insincerely play a part which represents experiences which they cannot imagine vividly.

A teaching manual will frequently suggest a play and give directions. Books of plays with music are also available, particularly for children.

Even twos and threes can act out God's care for flying or hopping birds, high-stepping horses, mooing cows, bleating sheep, or barking dogs.

Usually, for an older class to make successful use of dramatization, the teacher must be particularly interested in the method. Readers theater may be effectively used. This method of dramatic interpretation needs no props or costumes; the audience supplies all the details in their imaginations as two or more persons read a script.

DRILL

What It Is:

Drill is not merely memorization, although that is part of it. Nor is drill mere learning by rote or by rule. It is, instead, a learning process which furnishes automatic, recurring responses which will be helpful. Learning the books of the Bible in their proper order may be memorization, but it is also a means of helping the pupil to turn immediately to a desired Bible passage.

How to Use It:

Be sure that the lesson is within the pupil's understanding. The Junior child, for example, can read and handle his Bible and is ready to memorize the books of the Bible in their proper order. Some Primary pupils are not ready to memorize the books of the Bible, however, but can memorize hymns, Bible verses, and other appropriate material.

Accuracy of response must be maintained from the beginning. The Junior, for example, must be told how to pronounce correctly the names of the books of the Bible.

Repetition must be provided over a period of time with gradually lengthening intervals between drills.

FINGERPLAYS

What It Is:

The teacher tells a story to preschool children, using the fingers as characters in the story or parts of the scene. The children "play the story" with the teacher.

Action rhymes are related to fingerplays. But action is not limited to the fingers; the whole body can become involved. Action rhymes are helpful for young children who have not yet developed the use of small muscles.

How to Use It:

Make the fingerplay or action rhyme a part of the lesson. Make it contribute to the lesson aim.

Lay the groundwork for the fingerplay by using a story, a song, or a picture.

Speak slowly, using words and gestures carefully chosen to be within the understanding level of the pupils.

Keep the fingerplay short. Many are included as part of the lesson presentation in the teacher's book. These are quite appropriate for use.

End the fingerplay with eager, interesting inflection, perhaps as a surprise.

Watch the pupils carefully to make certain that everyone is able to understand and to participate.

HANDWORK

What It Is:

Handwork includes creative work done by the pupils such as freehand drawing, coloring, dot-to-dot drawing, cut-outs, stand-ups, patterns, posters, murals, sandtable figures, finger painting, clay modeling, and similar activities. Although older pupils learn by making replicas, maps, posters, banners, and Bible pictures, handwork is limited almost entirely to the children's department.

How to Use It:

Keep the handwork within the pupil's ability and understanding. The handwork guides, such as the teacher's book and activity packets, will be of help.

Two and three-year-olds can use blocks, pegboards, simple puzzles, and toys. They can even do simple pasting and coloring under close supervision. Beginners, ages four and five, do even better. Until the child is eight or nine years of age, handwork is particularly useful. Older pupils can make posters, murals, and do other similar art projects.

Plan far enough in advance to allow for the materials to be obtained and readied. A cupboard with shelving is necessary for storage. It needs to be high enough to be out of reach of the children.

Scissors with blunted ends are available for use by children. Do not use the ordinary kind of scissors.

Handwork is pleasure. Children do it at home as part of their play. When handwork is carefully planned for Sunday school, it reinforces the lesson while the children enjoy the activity.

Like all other methods, handwork should aid in the accomplishment of a definite teaching aim. It should not be used merely to keep the children occupied.

Children are extremely sensitive to recognition. The teacher should be generous with recognition.

Arrange for the handwork to be taken home to show to parents. However, an exhibit of handwork may be arranged from time to time for the benefit of the other teachers and workers, for the parents, and for interested relatives and friends.

MARCH OR RHYTHM

What It Is:

Young children require activity. March or rhythm is a good way to actively involve the children in expressing the teaching of the lesson.

How to Use It:

Use recorded music, piano, or clapping hands for accompaniment. The sorrowful mood is expressed by a slow walk, hands clasped in front, and head bowed. A contented, happy mood is represented by a quick walk or march. A joyful mood is expressed in a lively skipping fashion.

March or rhythm should contribute to the lesson aim. Prior to the action, the teacher creates the mood to be expressed by the use of pictures, stories, or tone of voice.

Activity choruses may also be used for Primary and Middler and Junior children.

MUSIC

What It Is:

Music may be used in a variety of ways to teach. Songs may be used to reinforce Bible concepts and facts. Older pupils may write new words, based on a Bible message, to existing music.

How to Use It:

Choose songs appropriate in words and range for the age group and lesson aim.

Use music to create moods, teach facts, or make application of the Bible truth.

PANEL DISCUSSION

What It Is:

Two or more members of the class, each fully informed and interested in one phase of a subject, discuss the subject while the other pupils listen.

How to Use It:

A panel discussion is best used in classes of teens or adults. The subject chosen should have as many phases as there are members of the panel.

The participants are to do research work, have notes in hand, and be adequately prepared to bring out all of the lesson teachings possible.

Choose pupils who can speak clearly and loudly enough to be heard by all.

Coach the participants carefully, making sure that each understands the lesson aim and that the contribution each is to make will apply definitely to the attainment of that aim.

Seat the panel where the participants can be seen and heard by everyone.

Warn the participants against merely talking with one another rather than presenting the material for which they are responsible.

PROBLEM

What It Is:

In math, the young learner begins with simple problems. "John had four apples. He gave one to Jim. How many did he have left?" As he advances in school, the problems become more complicated. In daily living he is called upon to solve all kinds of problems. In solving them he learns. In the Sunday-school class the teacher uses the problem solving technique to help the pupil to learn in the same way.

How to Use It:

Problems should be discovered by the pupils, not assigned by the teacher. Any assigned problem should be real-life.

Be on the alert for problem situations arising in class discussion. Utilize them by asking for solutions.

Plan puzzling questions that will lead to a live problem, awaken enthusiasm, create eagerness to solve the problem, and stimulate fruitful thinking. Keep the problem situations within the understanding and experience level of the pupil. (See the math problem above.)

See to it that the problem situation is related closely to the lesson purpose or aim. For example, if the lesson is "The Meaning of Discipleship," problems of all kinds may develop about the Christian's daily cross. Does it mean ill health? Domestic trouble? Financial distress? Keep it clear that Christian crossbearing is not a temporary situation, but an attitude that reaches into eternity.

Most problems arising in Bible study will be solved by reference to additional passages of Scripture. Teach the pupils how to find these references, make notes of them, and apply them in arriving at a solution.

The steps in solving a problem are four: (1) clearly state the problem, writing and rewording it until thoroughly understandable, (2) gather all information available bearing on the problem, (3) review this information, weigh it as evidence, and arrive at a solution, and (4) test the solution against every possible consideration to make sure it is flawless.

PROJECT

What It Is:

A project is putting a lesson aim into practice. Suppose that the purpose of the lesson is to encourage love for others. A child could try to help Mother by putting away toys after they are used. Juniors could run errands, shovel snow, mow lawns. Teens could visit shut-ins and conduct worship services or distribute gifts to the poor. Young adults could visit the inmates of public institutions such as the jail, hospital, or nursing home. Adults could collect gifts of money for someone in need, buy eyeglasses for children and aged persons unable to afford them, paint a widow's house, or a variety of other things.

How to Use It:

Most Bible classes have projects such as caring for a child in an orphanage, helping support a missionary, raising money for a building or other fund.

Such projects are excellent for expression.

Make it clear to the pupils that the project is the result of the Bible's teaching.

Enlist the pupils to help check all possible objections before a project is undertaken to make sure that it is agreeable.

Clearly outline the project on the chalkboard (if possible) with details of what, who, when, where, and why thoroughly understood and approved by every pupil.

Insofar as possible, have some project under way at all times.

QUESTION

What It Is:

A question reveals knowledge and provokes thinking. It is an inquiry, the act of asking. The teacher needs to know how to ask questions in a way that will stimulate and guide learning. He must also know how to answer questions in a way that will aid the pupil to learn. If the pupil does not think, he does not learn.

Jesus made frequent use of the question method, and His answers to questions are invariably effective, generally leading to more thinking and often to action.

How to Use It:

Use questions for the following purposes: (1) to help the pupil to understand what he knows and what he needs to know, (2) to arouse curiosity, stimulate interest, and develop purpose, (3) to direct attention to the important and away from the unimportant, (4) to lead the pupil to express his thoughts and thus to help you to guide his thinking, and (5) to ascertain what the pupil knows and thus decide what he needs to learn.

Plan your questions—and their correct answers—in advance. Make certain that the questions lead directly toward the achievement of the lesson aim.

Be sure that the question is complete and fully understood. Pupils are confused by questions which are incomplete or based on information which they do not have.

Answers should be complete and well-rounded, indicating that the pupil has a full understanding.

Questions should be of the kind that will create and maintain interest on the part of the entire class, not merely the more advanced pupils or the less advanced pupils.

Give the pupils plenty of time to answer. If they hesitate, perhaps the question should be reworded.

If only part of an answer is correct, accept that part with appreciation. Then proceed to clear up the rest of the answer. Do not leave any doubt as to what is the correct answer.

Encourage questions by the students. Sometimes a pupil's question may be more illuminating than the teacher's.

There are several kinds of questions: (1) factual—"In her song to Elisabeth, Mary gave several reasons why her soul magnified the Lord. What were they?" (2) interpretive—"What do you think Mary meant?" (3) application—"How do these several reasons apply to us?" (4) choice—"Which of these several reasons means most to you?" (5) reasoning—"Why?"

Study the Lord's use of questions: "For if ye love them that love you, what reward have ye?" "Is not life more than food?" Note how He led others to ask questions (Matthew 19:16-22).

REVIEW

What It Is:

A test or review is necessary for the teacher's evaluation of his teaching and of the pupil's learning. It has other advantages, too; such as helping the pupil to crystallize ideals, reinforce attitudes, revive interest, fix the lessons in memory, and make more of an effort to learn.

How to Use It:

Asking occasional questions during the lesson presentation is the accepted method of getting older pupils to help review the lesson.

A pupil can also participate in a review by preparing a summary at the close of a lesson, unit, or course.

WORKBOOK

What It Is:

The workbook contains questions and activities for the pupil to answer and problems and puzzles for him to solve under the teacher's supervision during the class session. The contents are discussed either prior to the use of the workbook, or afterward.

Usually workbooks, often called pupil's books, are available from the publisher who prints the teacher's manual and other supplies for the lesson course.

How to Use It:

A table, student chairs with arms on which to write, or clipboards must be provided along with pencils, color crayons, scissors, paste, or other materials required for use in the workbooks.

In older classes a pupil can help distribute the workbooks and necessary materials.

Keep the workbooks in a cabinet during the week. Keep extras on hand for visitors.

Refrain from giving a pupil too much workbook activity.

HOW TO SELECT THE METHOD TO BE USED

You have just examined thirty-six methods of impression and expression, each defined, with suggestions for using each. No teacher will use all of them in one lesson—or in many lessons, for that matter. With these thirty-six ways of making a lesson interesting and effective (and there are still more ways of teaching, not listed here), there is no excuse for any teacher to fall into the deadly rut of monotony in lesson presentation. No teacher should ever be like the one of whom a pupil said, "I know exactly how my teacher will begin next Sunday's lesson or the lesson a month from now, what he will say about it, and how he will end it. How can you be interested when the teacher doesn't even try to make the lesson interesting?"

No teacher will ever use all of these thirty-six ways of teaching in one lesson, but he ought to consider them, become acquainted with them, and use them on occasion. Here are some factors to be considered when choosing the methods to be used in a lesson.

1. *Would you like to try it?* The teacher must be enthusiastic if he wants the pupil to become enthusiastic.

2. *What is the lesson aim?* Is the method the best to accomplish that aim?

3. *What is the lesson content?* Is it a "story" lesson? A "question and answer" lesson? A "picture" lesson? A "tell and explain" lesson for the lecture method? Lessons differ, and this difference often makes one method better than another.

4. *Which method will appeal most to your pupils?* You will introduce them to new methods from time to time. In your teaching, you will discover which of them appeals most to your pupils. Your purpose, after all, is to help the pupils to learn. Therefore, keep them in mind.

5. *Do you have the facilities for the method you have in mind?* There is no use to decide to use a film, for example, if you do not have the necessary equipment or if the classroom does not lend itself to such a method.

6. *What method did you use last Sunday?* And the Sunday before? And the Sunday before that? Avoid monotony by using a variety of methods, but do not become a "methods addict," subjecting your class to something different all of the time.

7. *Do you have the time to use the method?* You have a very limited period of time during the class session. Use it to the best advantage. Do not waste precious moments with a method that takes more time than is justified. You are God's steward of the time in your class.

8. *Will it make the pupil desire to investigate?* The pupil's mentality must be stimulated, prodded, aroused to a keen interest in the truth being taught. Will the method stimulate such interest?

9. *Is the method adapted to the capacities and interests of the pupils?* You know the maturity of your pupils, Biblically speaking, better than anyone else. You know their capacities and interests. Is the method under consideration one which will be on their level of interest?

A SAMPLE PRESENTATION

The lesson topic was "Prayer in the Christian's Life" with a subtopic, "The Power of Prayer." It was the eleventh lesson in a quarter which had developed the general theme "Great Doctrines of the Church." The class was a group of fifteen men, meeting in a small room with every chair taken. The teacher stood with his back to a blank wall on which hung a chalkboard. A flannelgraph easel and board stood at the teacher's right and did not conceal the chalkboard.

The lesson text included the two familiar passages from Matthew 6:5-8 and 7:7-11 with James 5:13-16 added and 1 John 5:14 as the golden text. The lesson aim was obviously this: the pupil will be able to define prayer, understand it, and use it effectively.

Following is the presentation.

1. *Opening.* The teacher stood before the class, paused a moment, and said, "Let us pray. I shall lead in a brief prayer. Then let us unite in repeating together the prayer Jesus taught to His disciples, commonly called the Lord's Prayer."

2. *Main Points.* Next he explained that the lessons were a part of the theme "Great Doctrines of the Church" and gave the topic of the lesson for the day along with the aim. He told briefly of a man, a deacon in another church, who had asked him for a book or other information telling him how to pray. "Let's call this man John," he said, "although that isn't his name. In studying our lesson, let's learn the answer to his question about how to pray." He then introduced the various lesson texts, explaining their backgrounds and their relationship to each other. Then he said, "Now we shall read the text. Read it individually. Then we shall go back and review the text, finding the answer to the following five questions:

"Who is to pray, and to whom?"
"Why is he to pray?"
"When is he to pray?"
"Where is he to pray?"
"What is he to pray for?"

Watch now as we read and see if you can discover the answers to these questions."

The reading proceeded without interruption. The passages were then kept at hand, ready for reference, as the teacher asked the five questions. The men found the answers in the text, discussing each of them, and agreeing as to the teaching. The answers were written on the chalkboard as they were found. This occupied about three-fourths of the lesson period.

3. *Application.* The teacher explained that the deacon who had asked about prayer was a busy man who had many things which were likely to interfere with his daily living as a Christian. "Can you name some of the things that interfere with our faithful Christian living?" he asked. The men answered with suggestions. When they said, "Work" or "Money," a dollar sign was placed on the flannelboard. The answers came rapidly. Soon the teacher was able to make the point: "Yes, we have many interests in life. We need help to keep us faithful. That help is prayer."

He introduced one of the men who had a hardware store and asked the man to explain the difference between a thermometer and a thermostat. The man had a thermometer and a thermostat with him and explained the difference. The teacher thanked him and said, "Perhaps you know some 'thermometer people.' Every little discouragement makes them 'blue,' as we say. They are 'in the dumps.' But let something favorable to them come along and they are 'up in the clouds.' Their wives never know what to expect when they come home. Their friends and fellow workers cannot depend on them for they are never the same. As for their lives as Christians, they walk with one foot on the highway to Heaven and the other in the gutter leading to Hell. Up and down, here one Sunday and gone the next, unreliable 'thermometer men.' "

Holding up the thermostat, he told of "thermostat men"—those who pray faithfully and thus permit a power higher than themselves to regulate their lives' those who live according to God's will and not according to the temperature of the moment as do the "thermometer men."

He introduced a traveling salesman, a member of the class, and asked him, "When you are away from the home office and a problem comes along, what do you do?" Said the man, "I get in touch with the home office, and they tell me what to do." The teacher then likened the Christian as God's ambassador away from home and how he, like the salesman, keeps in touch with the "home office" for guidance, for encouragement, for strength. He then made the point, writing it on the chalkboard:

"When we read the Bible, God is talking to us.

When we pray, we talk with God."

4. *Closing* the lesson, he summarized briefly the points made, then called for a series of sentence prayers.

Notice the materials and methods used by this teacher.

Materials: Bible, chalkboard, flannelgraph, thermometer, thermostat.

Methods: Lecture, story, individual reading, question and answer, discussion, chalkboard, flannelgraph, object, and demonstration.

This lesson included a number of materials and methods, more than may be found in the usual lesson. There were probably too many. It may have been better if the flannelgraph or the object lesson had been omitted. However, this illustrates the variety of presentation devices which may be used with adults.

Note also that the materials and methods were what would appeal to men. Others would have been used had the class been composed of children, still others if the pupils had been teens and something different had those in the group been women instead of men. The teacher's presentation was directed to those in his class—men.

Notice, too, how the materials and methods developed the lesson aim to define, understand, and use prayer.

Had this presentation been a demonstration of teaching at a workshop, clinic, or other conference, the teachers present could gain much by discussing the teaching techniques used.

MY METHODS OF TEACHING BY EXPRESSION

or

Enlisting participation of my pupils

	I Use Often	I Use These Occasionally	I Should Use More	Inappropriate for My Use
Assignment				
Buzz Session				
Check Chart				
Collage or Montage				
Conversation				
Debate				
Discussion				
Drama				
Drill				
Fingerplays				
Handwork				
March or Rhythm				
Music				
Panel Discussion				
Problem				
Project				
Question				
Review				
Workbook				
Others:				

CHAPTER 10

MAINTAIN CLASSROOM CONTROL

You have prepared well. Now everyone in your class will be eager to learn. They will sit spellbound while you present the lesson. If you believe that, you are in for a rude awakening!

Teachers of children and youth will always experience the age-old problem of discipline. In spite of your most careful preparation, you will experience discipline problems emerging now and then. When discipline problems do occur, it isn't a signal to quit. Rather, it is evidence that you have real live pupils in your class!

The word discipline comes from the same root word as disciple. Disciplining, like discipling, is a growth process. Discipline is the process of helping an individual to learn self-control. When we discipline, we establish boundaries within which the child may operate. As he grows in self-control, we establish fewer boundaries for him because he is able to create his own. It is the teacher's responsibility to enforce boundaries of behavior fairly and consistently so the pupil may learn what is acceptable behavior and what isn't.

Discipline has been defined and applied in many different ways. Some teachers see it as punishment for crimes done, even to the point of retribution; some are vindictive when they administer discipline. However, we shall examine it from the preventive point of view, avoiding problems, and from a remedial view, restoring or remaking the misbehaving one.

CAUSES OF DISCIPLINE PROBLEMS

Physical Conditions

Physical conditions frequently are the culprits in behavior problems. A room which is either *too warm* or *too cold* is distracting. Adults go to sleep, but children move—and movement is generally the source of discipline problems.

Lighting—too dark to see or too much glare to be comfortable—affects classroom behavior. Younger pupils tend to try to get themselves into comfortable positions. Unable to do that, they often engage in disruptive behavior.

The *appearance of the classroom* itself affects behavior. A dirty, cluttered, unattractive room invites disrespectful, disruptive behavior. But an attractive, neat room elicits behavior in kind.

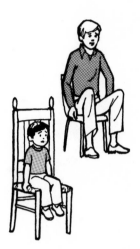

Outside noise also affects the behavior of children. It is distracting. When children's attention is diverted from the classroom activities, it is difficult for the teacher to regain attention.

The *size of the equipment* affects behavior. Little children who have to sit on chairs which do not fit them become restless, causing behavior disruptions. Anyone who is uncomfortable will seek to become comfortable—in either an acceptable or an unacceptable way. Many discipline problems would never have occurred if the equipment had been suitable.

Emotional Climate

Some discipline problems occur because of the emotional climate of the classroom. The emotional climate is very much the responsibility of the teacher. Check yourself in the following areas.

1. Do you demonstrate warmth and love in your relationships with each pupil? Pupils who fear you or don't think you care tend to be disciplinary problems.

2. Do you know each child well enough to be able to talk with him about his interests? Pupils seldom cause major disruptions when they know you care.

3. Do you expect the best from your pupils? Pupils generally respond to the expectations, either positive or negative, of the teacher. Of course, you will have occasional behavior problems even if you expect the best. But it is better to be surprised occasionally with negative behavior than to have only occasional pleasant surprises!

4. Do you establish reasonable behavior requirements for your pupils? For example, it is unreasonable to expect preschoolers to sit for an entire hour, but it is reasonable to expect them not to hit one another (although you may have to correct the latter behavior many times).

5. Do you enforce whatever regulations you do have fairly and consistently? Nothing confuses pupils more than for rules to be enforced rigidly for one person in one situation, then waived for the next person or the next situation.

6. Do you correct behavior firmly, but lovingly, preserving the personal integrity of the pupil? Ridicule and embarrassment should never be a part of the discipline pattern of the Christian teacher. Care enough to discipline, but at the same time, always care enough to do it lovingly and kindly.

You hold the key to the emotional climate of your classroom. Use it well.

The Home

Sometimes discipline problems occur because of home situations. Some children are never made to behave at home. Consequently, they don't want to behave at church either. Other children never get any attention at home. Therefore, they will do anything to get any kind of attention, positive or negative. You cannot eliminate the home situations, but you can learn about them and understand them in order to do what is best for the children involved.

Other types of home situations are only temporary in nature. The arrival of a new baby often disrupts the routine for a preschooler, leaving him with the need for additional attention. Changes in home routines may affect behavior. Good or bad news from home bears reporting by the child, and that may be a source of temporary disruptive behavior.

The only way that you can compensate for or cooperate with home situations is to know them. The only way you will know them is to visit in the home, get acquainted with parents, and work hand-in-hand with parents to help the child to learn self-control.

The Child Himself

Some behavior problems occur because of the nature of the child himself. Exceptionally bright and exceptionally dull pupils tend to become bored with routine activities. The very bright child may be quite advanced intellectually and, therefore, not challenged by the content and activities of the lesson. On the other hand, the very slow child may not be able to keep up with the activities of the other children. In both cases, the children are frequently socially inadequate, intensifying the behavior problems. Individualized activities and attention probably are the solutions.

Hyperactive children and mentally or physically handicapped students sometimes present special problems as well. Like those mentioned above, individualized activities and attention may be necessary. Knowing your pupils and their parents is essential.

Instructional Planning

Probably the most common cause of classroom discipline problems is inadequate instructional planning. It has been observed that some simple elements of classroom management and housekeeping will avoid discipline problems. The following factors may well be making or breaking your learning situations.

1. How adequately are you prepared? Thorough preparation is obviously essential. Chapter Seven developed that theme.

2. Do you arrive before the pupils do? That is important in order to prepare materials and arrange the room as you want it. Be ready to give undivided attention to the pupils when they arrive.

3. Do you have early activities planned for those who arrive before the official opening time for Sunday school? "Idle hands are the devil's workshop" goes an old saying. It is true in Sunday school. Have purposeful activities ready to introduce as the pupils arrive.

4. Do you use a variety of teaching methods? Chapters Eight and Nine have already introduced that topic.

5. Do you have materials arranged close at hand? Pauses to find materials or sort them out divert the pupil's attention.

6. Do you plan for changes of activities within the hour? Don't force pupils to sit for too long at one time. You may make them sit, but you can't force them to be attentive to the lesson.

7. Do you give attention to the seating of the pupils? Sometimes you will have two people who bring out the worst in each other when they are seated together. You can prevent that problem before it occurs.

HOW TO CORRECT BEHAVIOR

Whatever preventive measures you take will prevent many problems from ever arising; but no amount of preventive measures will eliminate every discipline problem. Don't be surprised by behavior problems. Just be ready to deal with them when they occur. A plan such as the one below may be helpful to you.

1. Decide if you must deal with the behavior or if you can ignore it. If you think the child is seeking attention and you can ignore it without disrupting the whole class, then ignore it.

2. If you must attend to the behavior, focus on the behavior. Continue to let the child know that he is acceptable, but that his behavior isn't. State what you saw. Let him agree or disagree.

3. Let the child know why he is being punished. Get him to state what he was doing which demanded punishment.

4. State what the acceptable behavior would be. Make this an instructive situation as well as a corrective one.

5. Make the punishment a natural consequence of the misbehavior. If a child misuses the scissors, then remove the scissors from him. If he disrupts the group, isolate him from the group.

6. After the child has been punished, be sure to reassure him of his personal worth to you. This need not be elaborate, but it does need to be done.

A plan such as this one will work in the vast majority of cases.

If classroom management were to be summed up in three words, those words would be: FIRM, FAIR, CONSISTENT. The guidelines in this chapter will help you to manage your classroom well—but only you can put the guidelines into practice.

Unit Three

Evaluate

CHAPTER 11

EVALUATE YOUR PUPILS

EVALUATION DEFINED

What is evaluation? Is it important? How do you do it?

When you evaluate anything, you make an appraisal of its merit or value. You may make this appraisal before you act, as in weighing the pros and cons of having cake or pie for dessert. Or you can make the evaluation afterward such as deciding after you have had dessert whether the cake or pie was good.

We have discussed teaching up to and including the lesson. Now let us evaluate. We must ask ourselves some basic questions just as a homemaker does after she has fed her family. She probably would ask three groups of questions:

1. How did the family like the food? What did they say? How did they act? What were the aftereffects? Did anyone get sick? Does the food help make a well nourished, physically fit family?

2. How about the ingredients? Were they correct? In the right proportion? Was the oven too hot or too cool? Was the pan of the right size? Was it attractive? Did I serve it correctly?

3. The homemaker also asks questions about herself. Did I mix the ingredients thoroughly? Could I have done better if I had tried harder? What did I do that I shouldn't have done? What did I fail to do that I should have done? What can I do better next time?

A prizewinning cook doesn't consciously ask herself these questions, but she does ask them just the same. She is constantly trying to do better by checking the oven, testing ingredients, observing the family's reaction. In other words, she evaluates in an effort to improve.

The Sunday-school teacher also evaluates, appraises, or checks, and constantly strives for improvement. That is one way he learns how to teach more effectively. Evaluation is just as necessary as thorough preparation or effective presentation. Indeed, it is a part of both thorough preparation and effective presentation.

The teacher asks:

1. *Regarding the pupils.* Did they learn? What were their reactions? Were they interested? Did they take part eagerly? Did they ask questions? Did their answers to questions reveal that they were learning? Are they growing spiritually?

2. *Regarding the presentation.* Was the lesson plan correct? Were the parts of the plan in the right proportion? Was the classroom or the environment conducive to learning? Were the methods used the right ones?

3. *How about me?* Did I work as hard as I should have worked on the lesson? What did I leave undone? What did I do that I should not have done? Was this lesson the most effective one I ever taught? If so, why? If not, why not? What can I do to make my teaching more effective?

The growing teacher evaluates (1) the pupil, (2) the lesson, and (3) himself. He does it consciously, prayerfully, making notes, keeping records for use in meeting a sacred responsibility. The report need not be for publication. No other human eyes need see it. It is known to God and to the teacher, but it will be reflected indelibly and eternally upon the hearts and lives of the pupils.

A PIOUS HOPE IS NOT ENOUGH

Let's face facts. Even in the public school, with its compulsory attendance requirements, its quizzes, tests, and examinations, evaluation questions are not easily answered. Surely a pupil can learn a fact. He can even learn how to use the fact. But does he use it? Does he use it properly? Is the knowledge of the fact and how to use it going to do him any good? The teacher must evaluate. But, of course, there is no guarantee that the student will use what he has learned.

How much more difficult it is then, to evaluate in the Sunday school where attendance is voluntary; where quizzes, tests, and examinations are seldom given for fear of driving the pupil away; where knowledge of a fact and how to use it is important; but where the pupil's attitudes, motives, loyalties, sense of values, and innermost life, known only to him, and to God are most important!

Too often a teacher hopes piously, and perhaps prays, that the pupil may have learned. Asked whether the pupils are advancing in favor with God, he replies, "I don't know, but I am praying for them."

Prayer is good, but it is not enough. The teacher must know whether the pupil is growing spiritually.

In order to teach effectively, the teacher must evaluate the pupil, his learning, his life. He must do this for several reasons:

1. The pupil's eternal destiny depends upon his Christian education. Jesus said, "By their fruits ye shall know them."

2. The teacher, helping in this Christian education of the pupil, must know the pupil's spiritual understanding and attitudes before he can measure his progress.

3. He must measure his progress in order to help him to learn what he needs to learn in order to grow spiritually.

122

4. His progress depends upon the teacher's teaching. Therefore, the teacher must know whether his teaching is effective, that is, whether his preparation is adequate and whether his presentation is getting results.

5. Since the pupil's advancement must be continuous, the teacher's evaluation must be continuous. The question is how the teacher evaluates the pupil's progress in Christian learning.

Educators suggest many methods of evaluation such as questionnaires, pupil placement tests, rating scales, score cards, life situation tests, conduct tests, attitude scales, descriptive records, autobiographical records, personality scales, character growth tests of various kinds, case studies, diaries, and others. All are good; some are excellent. They are described in tests and measurements books. But many are impractical for the Sunday school. However, perhaps a few suggestions as to methods will be sufficient here.

METHODS TO USE

For Children:

If the pupils are little children, the parents can help to evaluate their learning by answering the teacher's questions.

Some questions could be:

Is the child eager to come to Sunday school?

Does he ever tell you what he has learned?

Does he remember the lesson? (This can be answered by parents indirectly bringing up the subject at the Sunday dinner table.)

Does he get ready for Sunday school without urging?

Have you observed any change in his language, attitude, conduct, or interests which reflect the influence of the Sunday school?

Does he tell his playmates about his Sunday school?

Parents are accustomed to such check charts from public schools and are usually glad to participate in a survey. The questions can be sent home with the children with the request that they be returned the next Sunday. Or, better yet, make these questions the topic of conversation as you visit in the pupil's home.

For Teens and Adults:

A former teacher of a class of adults in Muskogee, Oklahoma, tried an end-of-the-year quiz in which his pupils gladly participated. A quiz sheet was given to each pupil to be checked and returned.

Dear Loyal Partners:

Please do not sign your name to this quiz!

That is not the purpose. Instead it is (1) to help each of us evaluate the year as individual Christians, and (2) to help me as your teacher to plan a teaching program for the coming year that will be more effective for the Lord's purpose. Thus, without knowing your name (and I repeat again—do not sign your name), I will know where to place the greatest emphasis in the Bible teaching program.

The four categories of Christian experience listed below were selected as being as nearly representative for the purpose of self-evaluation as could be done briefly. Give each one your careful consideration and indicate by placing an "X" or check in the box which most nearly describes your present position.

If, through your cooperation and provided the class as a whole helps me in this way, a similar quiz could be offered next year, and thereby determine the spiritual progress for these next twelve months.

The whole idea depends on the cooperation of every class member. The greatest value will be obtained if everyone will fill out a "Christian Quiz for the Year."

Sincerely,

CHRISTIAN QUIZ FOR THE YEAR

I. Worship Attendance

25 points ( ) Attended regularly.
15 points ( ) Attended more than half the time.
10 points ( ) Attended less than half the time.

II. Personal Prayer Life

25 points ( ) Personal prayers (return of thanks or otherwise) offered regularly all year.
15 points ( ) Personal prayers offered more than half the time.
10 points ( ) Personal prayers offered less than half the time.

III. Bible Reading

25 points ( ) Bible read regularly (not necessarily daily).
15 points ( ) Bible read more than half the time.
10 points ( ) Bible read less than half the time.

IV. Stewardship and Work

25 points ( ) Gave and worked each week—to the Lord's glory.
15 points ( ) Gave and worked more than half the time.
10 points ( ) Gave and worked less than half the time.

Score Yourself Before Turning In Your Quiz!

100 points is excellent.	The Lord is happy, too.
60 points or more.	You are on the right road.
40 points or less.	You better watch out!

The teacher said that his pupils made an overall grade of seventy the first time this quiz was conducted.

The following checklist for analyzing the pupil's participation in class sessions may help the teacher to learn how to deal with the individuals whom he is teaching.

Is the pupil:

A harmonizer: Encourages others by nodding in agreement. Settles arguments. Is friendly and warm. Praises others' ideas, agrees and accepts contributions of others.

An initiator: Suggests discussion topics. Presents new ideas and solutions. Keeps the group on the subject. Makes sure that everyone has a chance to participate.

A clarifier: Asks questions or elaborates on contributions of others to clarify for the group. Summarizes when necessary.

An information giver: Helps the group reach goals by offering personal experiences and opinions. Gives facts and other information when needed.

A listener: Serves as audience during group discussions. Shows interest by facial expression. Maintains participative attitude while talking very little.

Or is he:

An antagonist: Rejects ideas without consideration. Argues unduly on small points. Blocks progress by going off the subject. Quarrels with the group or individuals.

A dominator: Monopolizes conversation by not giving others a chance to participate. Lobbies for pet projects. Asserts authority; tries to lead the group; interrupts.

A clown: Disrupts the work of the group by horsing around. Jokes, mimics, calls attention to himself by exhibiting unusual behavior.

An apple-polisher: Tries to gain favor with the leader of the group or other members. Tears himself down or apologizes to gain support. Attempts to gain sympathy on personal problems.

A deserter: Refuses to participate. Sets himself aside from the group. Is indifferent, aloof, excessively formal, daydreams, doodles, whispers to others, wanders from subject.

MEASURING THE GROWTH OF MY PUPILS

0 absent.

1 pupil was present, nothing more.

2 pupil seemed interested.

3 pupil answered a question.

4 pupil made a comment.

5 pupil asked a question.

This kind of record should be made as soon after the class session as possible. The mark of five is the peak of participation. He seemed interested, of course, and he also probably answered a question and offered a comment, but the number in each case marks the apparent degree of interest and, therefore, to an extent, the degree of learning.

Pupil's Name	September	October	November	Evaluation End-of-Quarter

REMEMBER YOUR PURPOSE

Your measurement of the pupil's progress determines whether your purpose is being accomplished. That purpose is set forth in the Scriptures. As discussed in length in Chapter Two, it is twofold:

1. To recruit the pupil for Christ, leading him to an obedient acceptance of Jesus as the Son of God and as his personal Savior and Lord.

2. To conserve or nurture the converted pupil in Christian growth, or, as Paul puts it, "perfecting of the saints" (Ephesians 4:12, 13).

If your pupils are Junior level or above, review their progress by asking:

Does he believe in Christ?

If so, has he accepted Him?

Can he give evidences of Christ's claim to deity?

Can he explain the Scriptural requirements for becoming a Christian?

Can he outline briefly the plan of salvation revealed by God from Genesis to Revelation?

Can he define the church?

Can he give a brief history of the church from Pentecost to the present?

Too deep, you say? Too theological? Not at all if you, the teacher, have a clear understanding of the simple teachings of the New Testament. Indeed, many more questions could, and should, be asked concerning the ordinances, the requirements of the Great Commission, and the current issues of Christendom, including progress toward Christian unity.

Whether you are succeeding in the second objective of conservation or Christian growth of the converted pupil may be measured in part by observing whether:

He attends Bible class and other services of the church regularly.

He brings new members to the class and church.

He gives regularly with enthusiasm.

He participates in class and church activities generally, finding his chief interest in the church.

He observes daily devotions, including prayer and reading from the Bible.

He is generally admired as a Christian at home, school, work, and play.

His personal habits, conversation, and general conduct are those of a Christian.

He shows evidence of applying the Bible truths which the class has been learning.

Your purpose, remember, is to coach the pupil in his Christian growth. The suggested observations are superficial, of course, but by observing the pupil in these and in other ways, you can evaluate his progress to a degree.

Keeping in mind the characteristics of their age group, knowing what a child of a certain age ought to know and how he ought to behave, teachers of children can keep their own checklists. A record of this sort should be kept, for it is much more useful than a guess.

SOME ERRORS TO AVOID

Don't underestimate the importance of evaluation. The best teachers give a considerable amount of time for review, referring to past lessons, asking questions, testing the pupil's understanding of the present and past lesson in many ways.

Don't misunderstand the purpose of evaluation. The teacher is not merely checking on the pupil's progress, but also using the method as a means of instruction. Reviewing the lesson perfects the knowledge of the pupil, confirms this knowledge, and renders it ready for use.

Don't underevaluate. Teachers must not jump at conclusions based upon inadequate information. Be thorough. Consider all evidence obtainable.

Make evaluation continuous. The teacher reviews, questions, quizzes, tests, keeps records consistently, week by week, not just once a quarter.

Don't look upon evaluation as burdensome. The pupil is as much interested as the teacher. Methods of appraising progress are of interest to all. They are among the more interesting devices of learning.

Don't become dogmatic as regards information or method. A teacher who relies upon set methods of evaluation is going to miss the mark because pupils differ, situations differ, and even the same pupil is never the same.

KEEP A NOTEBOOK

Prepare an evaluation notebook. A good plan would be to have a page for each pupil with notes regarding his background, environment, personal characteristics, and other information. Also include a page for each quarter's record. It may be like the form below.

KNOWING MY PUPIL

Name _____

Address _____ Tel. No. _____

Date enrolled in school _____ In my class _____

Birth date_____ Member of church?_____

Dates of my visits to his or her home _____

Pupil's Sunday-by-Sunday Progress this Quarter	Comments Regarding Pupil

Special comments regarding pupil:

_____

_____

_____

_____

_____

CHAPTER 12

EVALUATE YOUR TEACHING

WAS IT A GOOD LESSON?

It is Sunday afternoon or evening. Your mind is on the lesson you taught this morning. You are asking yourself questions.

Was it a good lesson? That is, am I absolutely satisfied that it was all that it could have been? Did my pupils learn? Perhaps you close your eyes in silent prayer, asking the Lord to bless your pupils with a more complete understanding of His will for them and that the lesson of the day may find results in their Christian growth and living.

But you still wonder. Was it a good lesson?

You can find the answer to that question. As a growing teacher, you must find the answer to the question by reviewing your presentation of the lesson, by appraising your teaching. This is best done by keeping a notebook and developing a routine practice of checking each week's presentation. You may even prepare copies of a checklist and use one each Sunday. A review of these weekly checklists will reveal weaknesses and point the way to improvement. Several sample charts are provided in this chapter.

The checklist can follow the lesson plan you use, beginning with the aim and ending with the close of the lesson. Such a chart could be like this:

Date _____

Lesson Topic _____

Quarter's Theme_____

EVALUATING LESSON PRESENTATION

	Yes	No	Don't Know

Lesson Aim

Did I have a teaching aim clearly in mind?

Did I make it clear to the pupils?

Did I keep it clearly understood throughout the lesson presentation?

Do I believe the aim was accomplished?

Beginning the Lesson

Did I start the lesson on time?

Did the opening catch the attention of every pupil?

Was the opening true to the teaching aim?

Was it appropriate?

Was it pleasing to the pupils?

As an opening method would I say it was the best I could have used?

Main Points of Bible Study

Was each point clearly understood by all?

Were all the pupils interested?

Did I include one or more points that should have been omitted?

Did I overlook one or more points that should have been explained?

Did I give each point the amount of time it should have received?

Do I feel the Lord was pleased with the way I presented His holy Word?

Did I involve the pupils in the lesson?

Main Points of Application

Did each pupil understand how the teachings applied to his or her life?

Do I believe each pupil will do as taught?

Did I include one or more applications that should have been omitted?

Did I overlook one or more applications that should have been included?

Did I give each application the emphasis it ought to have had?

Do I feel the Lord was pleased with the way I applied His teachings?

Closing the Lesson

Did I close the lesson when I should?

Did the closing emphasize the teaching aim?

Did I finish all I had planned to say and do in presenting the lesson?

Would the pupils have enjoyed a longer lesson period?

Was the method of closing the best I could have used?

Do I believe every pupil will want to come back next Sunday because he believes my lessons are worth the effort?

130

On the next page of your notebook, you can include a checklist of the methods used, estimating the effectiveness of each. Such a checklist could be like this:

	My Evaluation of Its Effectiveness		
	Good	Fair	Poor
METHODS OF IMPRESSION (list those used)			
_____			
_____			
_____			
_____			
METHODS OF EXPRESSION (list those used)			
_____			
_____			
_____			
_____			

Using an ordinary 8½" x 11" notebook and attaching your lesson outline to the weekly appraisal, you can have a record to review from time to time to help you improve your teaching.

Allow space for comments by the pupils. Perhaps a pupil suggests a project which the class may undertake. You make a note of it. Then when a lesson is appropriate for such a project, you include it in your planning, giving the pupil credit for the idea. Or there may be a lack of reverence or a tendency toward cliquishness in the class. By writing down such observations and noting what you intend to do about them, you can follow a program of improvement that will change yours from an ordinary class into an extraordinary class.

The physical aspects of your classroom are also important to effective teaching. Good teachers make every effort to improve the environment. Following is a checklist for your use in evaluating the physical aspects of your classroom:

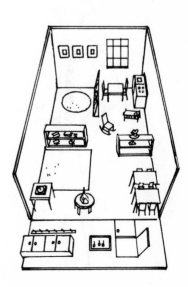

	Excellent	Good	Fair	Poor
(1) Lighting				
(2) Temperature				
(3) Ventilation				
(4) Quiet, no interruptions				
(5) Clean				
(6) Seats				
(7) Equipment				
(8) Arrangement of the equipment				
(9) Equipment graded to meet the needs of the group				
(10) Room left neat and clean with equipment properly arranged at close of class				

To teach well, you must speak well. Following is a speech rating chart. Although it is of the type used by a supervisor of teachers, it will help you to rate your own speaking ability. For each of the qualities of effective speaking indicated in this chart, check the line in the space which more nearly indicates what you believe to be your relative effectiveness as a speaker.

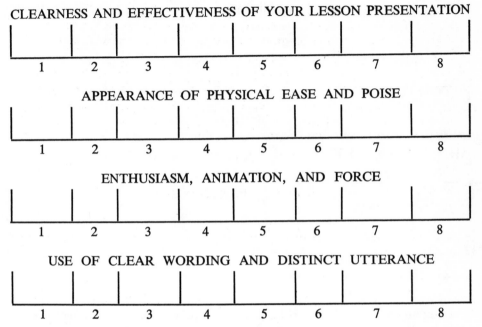

CLEARNESS AND EFFECTIVENESS OF YOUR LESSON PRESENTATION

| 1 | 2 | 3 | 4 | 5 | 6 | 7 | 8 |

APPEARANCE OF PHYSICAL EASE AND POISE

| 1 | 2 | 3 | 4 | 5 | 6 | 7 | 8 |

ENTHUSIASM, ANIMATION, AND FORCE

| 1 | 2 | 3 | 4 | 5 | 6 | 7 | 8 |

USE OF CLEAR WORDING AND DISTINCT UTTERANCE

| 1 | 2 | 3 | 4 | 5 | 6 | 7 | 8 |

Directions: In the space provided below, state one thing which you feel would definitely help your speaking to be more effective.

_____

_____

_____

Now, on the basis of your observations of your own speaking ability, check each weakness of speech which you think applies to your speaking, and work to correct it at once:

——*Monotonous voice.* (A speaker's voice needs to be animated with inflections denoting emphasis, right use of pauses, and other devices to avoid monotony and add to speaking effectiveness.)

——*Gestures weak, indefinite, or stiff.* (Naturalness in gesturing is best. The proper gestures can add much to storytelling or speaking, especially to children.)

——*Faulty grammar or pronunciation.* (These weaknesses are all too common.)

——*Frequently look at floor, ceiling, out the window.* (Look at the pupils.)

——*Peculiar mannerisms.* (It may be clearing your throat, jerking at your collar, leaning on the table or podium, rubbing your cheek, or a variety of others. Watch yourself, for there are many peculiar mannerisms, and they quickly become habits that distract the attention of the listener and detract from the effectiveness of your teaching.)

——*Wooden face*. (This is the face that never smiles or shows other emotion—"deadpan." You can train your facial expressions to help you teach. Do it!)

There are other faults, but this list is enough to help you to begin to evaluate your public speaking ability. Observe other speakers, note their attractive qualities, and be warned by anything in their speaking ability which may disappoint you. Try to make yours a "voice with a smile!"

The following line represents degrees of effectiveness, ranging from the left, which represents a presentation which would be likely to produce no response, to the right end, which represents a speech or story that should get the results you seek. Check the line at that point which indicates your relative effectiveness as a storyteller or speaker, as judged on the foregoing basis.

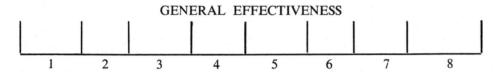

GENERAL EFFECTIVENESS

| 1 | 2 | 3 | 4 | 5 | 6 | 7 | 8 |

Then plan to correct your weaknesses and improve your ability!

Returning now to ways of evaluating the lesson presentation as a whole, a good way would be to check a lesson by the seven laws of teaching. Answer the questions below.

1. Did I thoroughly know the lesson I was to teach?

2. Did I gain and keep the attention and interest of the pupils, focusing the attention on the lesson aim?

3. Did I use words understood in the same way by the pupils and by me—language as clear and vivid to them as to me?

4. Did I begin with what is already well-known to the pupil and with what he has already experienced? Did I proceed from there to the new material in single, easy, natural steps, letting the known explain the unknown?

5. Did I stimulate each pupil's mind to action, leading him to anticipate what was coming next, letting him feel that he was discovering the thought for himself?

6. Did I require each pupil to reproduce in thought the lesson being learned, expressing it in his own language?

7. Did I review the past lessons, review the points in this lesson, and summarize them clearly so that no pupil was left with false understanding of the truth?

Remember, however, that your evaluation of your lesson presentation does not take place only when you check the chart. Such checking in a notebook as soon as possible after class may be a formal way of doing it, to be sure, but the presentation must also be evaluated at the time of teaching. The teacher knows whether a certain method is succeeding. If it isn't, he must be quick to change the approach and to alter the teaching in a way that will be interesting and effective.

If the pupils are old enough, they can help in the appraisal. (Evaluation, like every other part of teaching, changes in method with the age group.) A popular plan is for all of the teachers in the school to agree to have their work appraised by the pupils. Then under the direction of the departmental superintendents on a given Sunday, the pupils in the adult and teen classes take five minutes to check an evaluation chart. Without signing it or giving other identifying information, they turn the chart in for the guidance of the teachers. Following is one possible form.

STUDENT'S BIBLE SCHOOL CLASS AND TEACHER EVALUATION

Please underline what you consider to be the most accurate words or phrases within the parenthesis in each of the statements below. For the good of your class and teacher, please be perfectly honest. We are seeking to find the areas in which our Bible school can be improved. Your honest opinion will help. Please do not sign this paper or in any way identify yourself. Thanks!

1. I (have, have not) noted improvement in my teacher's teaching in the past six months.

2. My teacher's preparation (always, usually, seldom, never) seems quite adequate.

3. My teacher (does, does not) invite class discussion and (does, does not) allow enough opportunity for it.

4. My teacher (does, does not) emphasize the connection between lessons in a series from Sunday to Sunday.

5. My teacher (does, does not) usually hold my interest and attention through a whole lesson period.

6. My teacher (does, does not) seem genuinely glad to see me each Sunday morning.

7. I (always, usually, seldom, never) learn something worthwhile from my teacher's presentation of the Bible school lesson.

8. My teacher's teaching method (does, does not) stir me to independent thought on the subject or lesson being taught.

9. I (think, do not think) that a more active class social program would be beneficial to my class.

10. If for any reason I am forced to miss a Bible school lesson, I (would, would not) feel that I had missed very much.

11. (The activities of my class, The skills of my teacher) are such that I (am, am not) always proud to invite my friends to come to Bible school with me.

12. I think the time allotted for lesson study, if properly used, (is, is not) long enough.

13. Offhand, I (could, could not) tell anyone the main points in last Sunday's lesson.

14. My teacher (has, has not) made a call in my home within the last year.

Where teachers are being observed in instructor training schools other than the Sunday school, an observer usually fills out a form answering questions about the lesson presentation. The following questions are typical:

Was the aim clearly stated?

How was the attention gained?

How were the materials introduced?

What method of teaching was used?

Did the instructor stimulate thinking and discussion?

What teaching aids were used? How were they used?

Were questions specific and clear?

Were all students drawn into the discussion? Was the discussion related to the aim?

Which type of interaction predominated, the teacher-student or the student-student type?

How was the class control?

In what way did the teacher evaluate the outcome?

Did the teacher give assignments?

How did he summarize?

Did the teacher accomplish the aim?

Personal qualities of the teacher:

Poise?	Voice qualities?
Enthusiasm?	Attitude?
Preparation?	Personal appearance?

The beginning teacher may ask himself these questions:

How much interest did my pupils show?

What were the points of greatest interest?

What parts of the session were the dull spots?

What made the difference between the interesting and the dull points?

How many pupils took part in some way?

At what point was participation liveliest? Dullest? Why?

What did this participation reveal to me concerning the pupils who participated?

Did the presentation go as I had planned?

Which of my questions stimulated more interest? Which less? Why?

Did the application and the conclusion take hold of the pupils?

Did the lesson lead to action?

What have I learned about my teaching?

What improvements am I going to make next Sunday?

Indeed, if a teacher takes the time and makes the effort to consider carefully the last two questions, answering them with a sincere desire and determination to be a better teacher, the evaluation will be profitable.

Following is a chart used by supervisors in a technical training school to check the work of teachers in training and to grade their effectiveness. Perhaps you can grade yourself by using this chart. Then you can learn where improvement is needed.

LESSON DESCRIPTION
(Brief description of activities as they occur)

FACTOR ANALYSIS
(a—superior, b—average, c—below average, d—inadequate)

1. Student readiness a b c d	13. Training aids—maximum appropriate utilization a b c d
2. Student attention a b c d	14. Continuity of lesson a b c d
3. Student cooperativeness a b c d	15. Summaries—effectiveness and timing a b c d
4. Student participation a b c d	16. Appreciation of student effort a b c d
5. Student reasoning for themselves a b c d	17. Effectiveness of speech a b c d
6. Student respect for instructor a b c d	18. Eye contact a b c d
7. Classroom atmosphere a b c d	19. Enthusiasm and interest displayed by instructor a b c d
8. Questions—adequate number a b c d	20. Patience a b c d
9. Questions—effectiveness a b c d	21. Emotional fitness and sincerity a b c d
10. Clarity of explanations a b c d	22. Appropriateness of appearance a b c d
11. Evaluation—frequency of a b c d	23. Knowledge of subject a b c d
12. Evaluation—effectiveness of a b c d	24. Instructor's poise a b c d
	25. Lesson plan a b c d

The concluding thought is this. Sometimes the very best evaluation is done when you are talking over these questions and their answers with God in prayer.

CHAPTER 13

EVALUATE YOURSELF

"TAKE HEED UNTO THYSELF"

"Thou therefore which teachest another, teachest thou not thyself?" (Romans 2:21). "Take heed unto thyself, and unto the doctrine; continue in them: for in doing this thou shalt both save thyself, and them that hear thee" (1 Timothy 4:16).

You may spend hours evaluating your pupils until you know exactly what each has learned and needs to learn. You may add more hours of evaluating the lesson presentation until you know the techniques of teaching and are a master of pedagogy and psychology. You may be put on a pedestal and be acclaimed the teacher of the year. But if you do not measure up to Christian standards in your own life, you are a failure as a teacher.

Perhaps more important than anything else, therefore, is your evaluation of yourself: your inner life, your constant appraisal of that which is known only to God and to you, and your prayerful, persistent effort to improve. To help in that improvement, you probably appraise yourself by asking questions such as:

Did I give enough time to preparing the lesson?

Did I pray about the lesson and look to God for help?

Did I do my best?

These are good questions. All good teachers ask them and arrive at the answers. But to help you to become a more thorough analyst of yourself, here are more questions, more tests, more guides for your thinking as you attempt to continually improve your teaching.

MY JOB AND I

To check your qualifications and your success in your job in the church's Sunday morning Bible school, put an "X" in the "yes" or "no" column, or put a number from 1 to 4 in the "partly" column after each question. Then multiply the number of "yes" marks by 5, add the number in the "partly" column, and you have your grade.

	Yes	No	Partly

A. I Am a Worker for the Lord

1. As a Christian, I am a worker for the Lord.
   Am I doing the work for which I am best fitted?

B. My Evaluation of My Spiritual Qualifications

2. Am I thoroughly committed to the Christian work entrusted to me, willing to make the sacrifices necessary for success?

3. Am I an active, supporting member of my local church?

4. In my home life am I a Christian, as shown in my relationship with the members of my family, my daily reading of God's Word, meditation and prayer?

5. In public are my dress, words, actions, and general behavior such as to bring honor to my Lord?

C. My Evaluation of My Improvement in My Job

6. Have I taken the elemental training courses pertaining to my work in the church Sunday school?

7. Am I continuing to improve myself as a worker, by further training?

8. Do I own and use a personal library pertaining to my work?

9. Do I practice self-development through individual reading and study?

10. Do I practice self-development through observation, visiting other schools, attending laboratory classes and demonstrations?

D. My Evaluation of My Ability as a Leader

11. Do I make the best use possible of suggestions from the head of my department in the Sunday school?

12. Am I on friendly and cooperative terms with the other workers in my church and its Sunday school?

13. Am I reliable, dependable, trustworthy?

14. Am I constantly on the lookout to discover and help train new workers in the church and its school?

15. Are my motives in my work above criticism?

E. My Evaluation of My Efforts

16. Do I devote at least one hour to my work each week, not counting Sunday or the time given to preparation for Sunday?

17. Am I always fully prepared for my work on Sunday morning?

18. Am I present at least fifteen minutes early on Sunday morning?

19. Do I make it a rule to begin and to stop exactly on time in my Sunday morning session?

20. Am I satisfied that I am doing my best in the work for which I have been selected?

Total _____

My Grade is _____

MY CHARACTER

Your character is important to your work as a teacher. If you are to develop Christian character in your pupils, you must possess in your own life those characteristics which you desire to develop in others. Here are some questions designed to help you to judge your own character. What are your strong qualities? What are your weaknesses? Check those where improvement is needed.

Are You . . .

Or Are You . . .

Are You . . .	Or Are You . . .
1. Open-minded, inquiring?	Narrow, not hungry for truth?
2. Accurate, thorough, discerning?	Indefinite, superficial, lazy?
3. Judicious, balanced, fair?	Prejudiced, led by likes and dislikes?
4. Original, independent, resourceful?	Dependent, imitative, subservient?
5. Decisive, possessing convictions?	Uncertain, wavering, undecided?
6. Cheerful, joyous, optimistic?	Gloomy, morose, pessimistic, bitter?
7. Amiable, friendly, agreeable?	Repellent, unsociable, disagreeable?
8. Democratic, broadly sympathetic?	Snobbish, self-centered, exclusive?
9. Tolerant, humorous, generous?	Dogmatic, intolerant, selfish?
10. Kind, courteous, tactful?	Cruel, rude, untactful?
11. Tractable, cooperative, teachable?	Stubborn, not able to work with others?
12. Industrious, forceful, vigorous?	Uncertain, weak, not capable?
13. Modest, self-effacing?	Egotistical, vain, autocratic?
14. Courageous, daring, firm?	Overcautious, weak, vacillating
15. Honest, truthful, frank, sincere?	Dishonest, hypocritical?
16. Patient, calm, equable?	Irritable, excitable, moody?
17. Regular, punctual, on-time?	Tardy, usually behind-time, incapable?
18. Methodical, logical?	Haphazard, inconsistent?
19. Poised, erect in posture?	Discomposed, sluggish in posture?
20. Constant and earnest in prayer?	Cold, formal, negligent in prayer?
21. Feeling a religious certainty, peaceful?	Under conflict, strain, uncertainty?
22. Expanding your religious life?	Static in your spiritual life?
23. Desiring to win others?	Little concerned for the lost?
24. Interested in the Bible?	Little concerned for God's Word?
25. Deeply confident in the Bible?	Doubtful of portions of God's Word?
26. Fully consecrated to the Lord?	Reserving part of your life for self?
27. At peace with God?	Unrepentant?
28. Born again?	Only a church member trying to do good?

Continuing the personality profile test for you to make of yourself as a teacher, here is another. Check after each question your estimate of your possession of the quality. If you check 1 or 2, you are below average. If you check 3 or 4, you are average. If you check 5, you are superior.

Quality	Definition of Quality	Your Estimate				
		1	2	3	4	5
Sincerity	Being true or genuine, honest, upright					
Loyalty	Faithfulness to country, friend, promise or duty					
Enthusiasm	Intense interest, zeal, earnestness					
Willingness	Cheerful readiness to perform assigned duties					
Cooperation	Being able to act or work with others toward a common end					
Self-confidence	Feeling sure that your ability is equal to demands					
Personal Appearance	Being well-groomed, presentable in dress and cleanliness					
Health	Possessing satisfactory physical condition for the job to be done					
Forcefulness	Using adequately firm and decisive action and expression					
Emotional Stability	Ability to maintain poise under emotional stress					
Tactfulness	Saying and doing what is effective or suitable in given circumstances					
Courtesy	Being polite, kind, and considerate					
Friendliness	Being cordial and kind					
Persistence	Ability to continue in spite of adverse conditions					
Patience	Willingness to repeat, restate, and redo as often as time will permit in order to help pupils understand					
Good English	Using words effectively in clear, thoughtful expressions					
Good Voice	Having a pleasing voice, strong enough to be heard but not irritating					

THE DIVINE EVALUATION

Bible in hand, you can evaluate yourself as a teacher by noting the divine references to your responsibility. There are many such references, for the teacher and teaching are prominent in the Lord's work. The following are not all of the references to teaching, for a one-volume concordance gives two hundred and nine references to taught, teach, teacher, and teaching, in addition to the references to servant, child, children, growth, and others that could be included. These, however, are typical.

As to Purpose:

Evangelism—Matthew 28:19.
Nurture—Matthew 28:20.
Developing perfect people—Ephesians 4:13.

As to Qualifications:

Faithfulness—2 Timothy 2:2.
Ability to teach—2 Timothy 2:2.
Humility—1 Corinthians 1—4.
Exemplary life—James 3:1-18.
Sound in the Scripture—Titus 1:9.

As to Lesson Preparation:

Using God's power—2 Corinthians 4:7.
Taking heed to the doctrine—1 Timothy 4:16.
Discerning—Hebrews 5:12-14.
Growing in grace and knowledge—2 Peter 3:18.
Studying the Bible—2 Timothy 2:15.

As to Lesson Presentation:

The right attitude—2 Timothy 2:14, 16-18, 21-26.
The right motives—1 Timothy 3:5.
Persistence and patience—2 Timothy 4:1-5.
Temper teaching with love—1 Corinthians 16:14.
Begin the lesson properly, noting how Christ began—Matthew 5, how Peter began—Acts 2, how Stephen began—Acts 7:2, how Paul began—Acts 22:3; 26.
Present the Bible as God's Word—2 Peter 1:16-21.
Apply its teachings to life. (One book of the Bible—the book of Acts—tells how to become a Christian. The following twenty-one books tell how to live as a Christian.)
Make the conclusion personal and decisive—Acts 26:29.

As to the Final Grade:

Teacher, beware!—James 3:1 *(NASB)*

WHAT EDUCATION DO YOU NEED?

The director of education in the local church is one who counsels with teachers, observes their work, and makes recommendations for improvement. If such a person were to sit in your class and observe your teaching, he would try to find the answers to some key questions. You can be your own supervisor, evaluating yourself and conducting a personal program of improvement. The director's questions, which you ask of yourself and by yourself, would be similar to these:

Some teachers have more natural ability than others; they are "apt to teach" (1 Timothy 3:2, 2 Timothy 2:24). Is this teacher one who is "apt to teach"?

Does this teacher fit the age group to which he has been assigned? Or should he be teaching pupils of another age?

Would this teacher make a better worker in some capacity other than teaching?

Is there another teacher available for this class who is more capable than this teacher?

What education has this teacher had in Bible content? In pedagogy? What education does he or she need?

Is this teacher one who is willing to study in order to become more effective?

He would seek the answers to questions about your lesson preparation and presentation, your characteristics, your acceptability according to the standards set by God's Word, and others, all of which have been asked in other tests suggested in this chapter.

Another good way to continue to evaluate yourself is to read good books and magazine articles on teaching and to make a comparison with the standards set forth there. A visit to another class to observe an experienced instructor teach pupils the same age as yours, whether in Sunday school or the public school, offers an excellent basis for evaluation. So does attendance at clinics, seminars, and demonstrations.

To invite another teacher to sit in your class from time to time and honestly appraise your teaching is often a helpful and revealing experience. Young teachers, especially, could benefit by doing this. An increasing number of Sunday schools now include some observers to visit classes and later confer with the teachers.

If you sincerely desire to improve your ability as a teacher, these and other methods of evaluation will be a continuous part of your program. In the final analysis, however, the product, which is the pupil, is the determining factor. As the Master said concerning teachers, as well as others, "By their fruits ye shall know them" (Matthew 7:20).

LEADER'S GUIDE

This section is the Leader's Guide. It is for you, the leader, who will guide prospective and experienced teachers into teaching with success.

The preceding thirteen chapters of *Teach With Success* are your wellspring of successful teaching ideas. In this guide you will not find quantities of new information to pass on to your students. But you will find lead-in ideas, activities, discussion questions, and visual aid suggestions that will prepare students to become better teachers in and out of the classroom.

GOALS: As a leader, you should have a good idea of what you want to see happening in your students' lives. These goals will provide a definite plan for bringing changes, and a way to know when those changes have taken place. Select two or three of them for each class session. They will give direction to your planning and evaluation to your teaching.

EXCITE: One or two activities will involve your students in each learning session. Enter in excited and your students will be properly motivated and become enthusiastic. Most activities are designed for groups, thus creating more learning from a variety of experiences.

An estimated time is given for each section bringing the total amount of time for each teaching session to sixty to seventy minutes. Excite has the added advantage of using Entry Time. (Entry Time (ET) is the extra minutes before class which can be used when the first student arrives.)

TRANSITION SENTENCE: The transition sentence(s) between Excite and Explain is the single most important sentence of each session. This sentence(s) connects the beginning activity with the remainder of the lesson. Worded precisely, it is designed to bridge what has been learned to what will be learned.

EXPLAIN: Using the Scriptures or *Teach With Success*, class participants will engage in learning activities to discover for themselves truths about teaching.

Your responsibility in guiding others to successful teaching may be greater than you think. Students may follow your example in *their* classroom. Is your example a mirror of *what* you teach?

EXPLORE: In this section students will be involved in practical application: **How** will they best get the message across? **What** will they do with their new information? You must help them evaluate their potential and talent for teaching and determine how they best can glorify God.

EXPAND: Students are now ready to make specific plans for their present or future classroom situations. These plans should reflect the truths learned in the class session.

EXECUTE: More than just an assignment, this section will take the learning right into the classroom. Participants will start with an observation of a teacher and conclude with teaching a class. As a leader you will be responsible for obtaining one-time teaching opportunities for each of your students (between lessons 12 and 13). Volunteer to arrange any other assignments, too.

LESSON 1

Know Yourself

Goals: Each pupil should be able to:
1. *Locate* Bible references which affirm the ministry of teaching.
2. *Identify* characteristics in teachers who effectively influence lives.
3. *Evaluate* his own life in light of those characteristics.
4. *Devise* a personal plan to work on areas in his own life which need improvement.

Materials: Paper, pencils, Bibles.

Excite *(ET plus 10 minutes)*

Before the pupils arrive, place a graffiti poster on the wall. (Shelf paper or table paper will be fine.) Write on it: "A good teacher is. . . ." Place felt markers nearby. As the pupils enter, direct them to determine an answer and write it on the poster. When a student has written his answer, give him the following directions.

On this piece of paper draw a large circle; in that circle draw a smaller circle and label it "Me." Draw and label other circles to represent people who have influenced your life. Those with the greatest influence should be placed nearest to "Me."

When most participants have completed the activity, let them share who influenced their lives and why. Place the "why" responses on the chalkboard. (If this is a typical group, the responses will reveal that people influence others by verbal input, confronting, caring, and modeling. If not, add such comments.) Read through the graffiti responses.

TRANSITION SENTENCES: Who is an effective teacher? What does the Bible say about teaching? Can you be an effective teacher? Let's find out.

Explain *(30 minutes)*

Give the class members the following questions. Instruct them to use Chapter One in *Teach With Success* and their Bibles to discover the answers. Let them work in pairs.

1. What evidence in the New Testament points out the need for and place of teaching?

2. What is the purpose of teaching in the New Testament?
3. What are the personal obligations of the teacher?

(Allow 10 to 15 minutes for research and discussion.)

Summarize the material in Chapter One dealing with the qualifications of a teacher. Illustrate your lecture with a strip chart. (All of the points of your lecture are placed on the chart and covered with strips of paper. As you develop each point, reveal it by removing the strip.)

Explore *(25 minutes)*

Ask pupils: *Think of the worst teacher you ever had anywhere. What made the teacher ineffective?* List characteristics on the chalkboard.

In the same way compile a list of characteristics of the best teacher they ever had. Compare the two lists. Point out that the effective teacher is committed to his subject, models behavior, prepares well, and relates well to his pupils.

Can you become an effective teacher? You can, if you attend to the development of your own personal life. Allow time for students to evaluate themselves by completing the charts: "Advance in Favor With God," "Advance in Favor with Men," "Personality Profile Test," and "My Mental Checklist." Instruct them to select an area from each chart to make priority items for self-improvement.

What rewards may a teacher expect? Ask those pupils who have been involved in any kind of teaching ministry to share the rewards they have experienced. Share your own testimony as well. Refer to the rewards identified in Chapter One.

Expand *(5-10 minutes)*

Read Luke 6:39, 40. Say, *"An effective Christian teacher relates well to others. He is a model for the Christian life. What will it require in your life for you to become an appropriate model as a teacher? You have selected some areas during your evaluation; if you haven't written them down, please do so now."*

Assign the pupils to triads (groups of three). Ask each individual to share with the others in his triad what he must do to become an appropriate model. After everyone in the triad has shared, each person is to pray for the individual on his right, asking God to strengthen and guide that person to do what he must to become an effective teacher. As each triad finishes, call your students' attention to the assignments for next week and dismiss them.

Execute

1. Read Chapter Two in *Teach With Success* for next week.
2. Observe a teacher in action. Decide if he demonstrates effective or ineffective characteristics and why.
3. Work on those areas of your own life which you decided need improvement; develop your spiritual and intellectual resources.

LESSON 2

Know Your Purpose

Goals: Each pupil should be able to:
1. *Identify* the two-fold purpose of teaching in the church.
2. *Locate* Scripture references which set forth the purpose of teaching in the church.
3. *Evaluate* the value of his own involvement in the two-fold purpose of teaching in the church.
4. *Commit* himself to fulfilling both purposes for Bible teaching.

Materials: Newsprint, felt pens, crayons, mimeograph or typing paper, Bibles, pencils.

Excite *(ET plus 10-15 minutes)*

As the pupils enter, assign them to groups of four to six to discuss the question, "What should a Sunday-school teacher accomplish? What is his goal?" Let the group summarize the discussion by designing a cartoon strip.

Direct the groups next to identify things they have learned in Sunday school or some other Christian education setting such as youth groups, camps, vacation Bible school, or a Bible study. This may be content, attitudes, or how to do something. As the groups brainstorm, have the reporters list the answers on a sheet of newsprint. Listen as the group reporters present their findings. Be ready to summarize their ideas into categories that you can write down. If the results are typical, you will be

able to point out that the pupils have learned facts, skills, feelings, attitudes, and behaviors. Some were learned before becoming a Christian, others after becoming a believer.

TRANSITION SENTENCE: *What does the Bible say your purpose is? Let's find out.*

Explain *(20 minutes)*

Put the following Scriptures on the chalkboard: Matthew 28:19; Mark 16:15, 16; Luke 24:47, 48; Acts 1:8; Ephesians 4:12-16. Direct the pupils to find the answers to the following questions:
1. What are the two main purposes of the church? (Evangelism and nurture.)
2. How does teaching help the person who is already a believer? (Perfects the saints, encourages pupils to ministry, instructs those in the church, brings unity, urges pupils to be Christlike, helps pupils to know what they believe and why, and shows how to behave as a Christian.)

Let each person work individually to answer the questions. Then let the pupils share their answers. List these on the chalkboard. Summarize.

Explore *(20 minutes)*

If the purpose of Bible teaching is for evangelism and nurture, how does that apply to you? Maybe you teach preschoolers. How, then, can you implement both goals? Even if you do teach preschoolers, and even if it will be some time before your preschoolers are ready to become Christians, you are still teaching for evangelism and nurture. You are laying the foundations with information, attitudes and feelings so that one day the child is ready to become a Christian. You have taught for evangelism, but you have adjusted your expectations as to when the results may be seen.

Your purpose, then, is to teach to change the way people act. Find Colossians 1:9, 10. Read it. There Paul tells how to teach. He begins by saying that we teach knowledge–facts. But we don't stop there because the pupil must understand the meaning of the facts. Even that isn't enough, for the pupil must then know how he can use the information to follow Jesus. And even then, you aren't finished, for the pupil must commit himself to do something as a result of receiving the material. (See Richards, Creative Bible Teaching.) A good Bible lesson always follows the complete cycle–knowledge, understanding, implications for action, and commitment to action. That is your purpose as a teacher.

How are you doing? Check yourself. Turn to Chapter Two in Teach With Success. Rate yourself in your work of evangelism and nurture. (Let the pupils tally their own scores.)

Divide the class into groups of six to discuss for three minutes the question, "How can you carry out your dual purpose of evangelism and nurture?" Then record their answers on the chalkboard.

Expand (5-10 minutes)

Summarize today's Bible lesson. Then briefly challenge the pupils to actively involve themselves in the twin work of evangelism and nurture.

What will you do to carry out the work of evangelism and nurture? It is up to you to decide. Write your prayer to God to promise to do whatever you feel you can and should do for God. After the prayers have been written, have a time of silent prayer.

Execute

1. Read Chapter Three in Teach With Success.
2. Observe a Bible class. Decide what purposes the teacher is trying to accomplish. Are they appropriate for the class? Is the teacher doing it well?
3. Plan a way to carry out your commitment to evangelize and nurture.

LESSON 3

Know Your Pupils

Goals: Each pupil should be able to:
1. Identify the age divisions in the typical Sunday school.
2. Identify the general characteristics and needs of each age division.
3. Describe the specific characteristics of specific pupils in his class (or one he observes).
4. Determine a general plan of teaching action to meet the needs of the particular age group he teaches.

Materials: Shelf paper, poster paper, construction paper, coat hangers, crayons, felt pens, glue, pencils, Bibles, yarn.

Excite (ET plus 10 minutes)

As the pupils enter the room, direct them to the first page of Chapter Three in Teach With Success. Have them fill out the information on at least three people in their classes. (If they aren't teaching a class, have them choose three people on whom to do the profile.) When they have finished, let them share in groups of two or three people.

How would you describe a four-year-old to someone who didn't know what he was like? Or a teenager? A forty-year-old? See how well you can do with that assignment. Draw up a description of what you might generally expect of each age group. Have them continue to work in groups of two or three. Let each group share their findings.

TRANSITION SENTENCES: If we are to teach effectively, we must know what to expect from our pupils, whatever their ages. That is our goal for today.

Explain (35 minutes)

Man is made by God. He is wonderfully and fearfully made, the Bible says (Psalm 139:14). He is made just a little lower than God, again the Bible reveals (Psalm 8:5 and Hebrews 2:7-9, *NASB*). God made man a unique person, able to think and love and feel like God. Yet there are similarities between people at particular age levels. It is the similarities, as well as the differences, which every teacher must understand.

Sunday schools commonly divide pupils into specific age groups: crib babies, up to age 1; toddlers, age 1; twos and threes, ages 2 and 3; beginners, ages 4 and 5; primaries, grades 1 and 2; middlers, grades 3 and 4; juniors, grades 5 and 6; young teens, grades 7 through 9; senior highs, grades 10 through 12; young adults, 18 through 24; and adults, above 24. Display this on a chart.

Divide the class into age group interests. If your class is small, have a preschool, children, youth, and adult section. If it is large, you may have duplicate sections—or you may have crib babies, toddler, twos and threes, beginner, primary, middler, junior, young teen, senior high, and adult groups. Direct each group to do the following:

1. Review age-group characteristics for your age group in Chapter Three of *Teach With Success*.
2. Add any other characteristics you think should be on the list.
3. Choose the five most important characteristics for you as a Bible teacher.
4. Illustrate your choices. (Assign groups to illustrate by writing a song, making a mural, creating a mobile, doing a role play, making a poster, and/or preparing a television interview. Assign a different activity to each age group.)

Share the findings. Add any observations of your own.

Explore (15 minutes)

What does all of this mean to you as a Bible teacher? Will knowing these general characteristics help you to teach them? How? Will knowing your pupils in general substitute for knowing each one individually? How can you get to know your pupils individually? How would you begin a class with them?

Continue to work in the same groups to answer these questions. Have them keep a record of their suggestions. Choose someone from each group to report. Add anything you feel should be covered.

Expand (5-10 minutes)

You never teach into a vacuum. You always relate the Word of God to people who are very much alike, yet quite different. There is no substitute for getting to know your pupils and planning to utilize their characteristics to teach them effectively. We began by describing three pupils. Maybe you could do it easily. Perhaps you need to know your pupils better. Why not write a letter to one of those individuals in which you tell him how you will get to know him better and how you will try to teach to meet his needs and characteristics.

After the letters are completed, let each person share with one other person. Let those two pray together to finish the class session.

Execute

1. Read Chapter Four in *Teach With Success*.
2. Observe an individual of the age group of your choice. How does he fit the textbook description? In what ways does he differ?
3. Try, formally or informally, to teach a Bible truth (a fact, a skill, a feeling) to an individual of the age group of your choice. Did he learn? How did he learn? What would you do the same if you were to teach him again? What would you do differently?

LESSON 4

Know Your Subject

Goals: Each pupil should be able to:
1. *Cite* at least two reasons for studying the Bible.
2. *List* the steps of effective lesson preparation.
3. *Identify* helpful tools for lesson preparation.
4. *Evaluate* his own study habits.
5. *Make a plan* for developing a personal library.
6. *Commit* himself to following the steps and discipline necessary to prepare effectively.

Materials: Index cards, magazines with pictures, glue or paste, felt pens, shelf paper, Bibles, pencils, poster paper, concordance, Bible dictionary, Bible atlas, translations of the Bible, hymnal, grammar, and teacher's book.

Excite *(ET plus 10 minutes)*

As the pupils enter, give them an index card with the following statements on them. Each pupil is to mark **agree** or **disagree** by each statement.
1. The Bible is a unique book, different from any other ever written.
2. Only one person wrote the Bible.
3. We have the Bible in order to tell man of God's plan for him.
4. The purpose of Bible teaching is to help the pupils to learn and to practice what God wants them to know and to do.
5. The Bible is the chief textbook in the Sunday school.
6. Nothing but the Bible should be used in the Sunday school.
7. The teacher of the Bible should prepare carefully in order to teach.

After the pupils have completed their work individually, let them then make a list of all the reasons they can think of to study and teach the Bible.

Explain *(35 minutes)*

TRANSITION SENTENCES: *Why do we need to know our subject? Because the Bible is God speaking to us. Because God's Word, believed and practiced, transforms lives. Because only God's Word can transform lives. Because of many other reasons you have listed.*

Using your lists and 2 Timothy 3:16, 17, make a collage to demonstrate why it is important for the teacher to know the Bible and to help others to know it. Let the pupils work in groups of four to six to make a collage. When they have finished, let them share what they have done. Display the finished products on the wall.

How can we come to know our subject? Prepare a display of Bible study helps—concordance, commentary, Bible dictionary, Bible atlas, various translations of the Bible, hymnals, English grammar, teacher's book, and other helps. Show these to the pupils. If needed, demonstrate briefly how to use them.

How, then, do you go about preparing a Bible lesson? Review the five steps of lesson preparation from this book. Use a poster to keep the points before the pupils.

Explore *(15 minutes)*

Let's see how we do. First, let's try our hands at using the Bible study tools. Let's suppose we are teaching a Bible lesson in which Jericho is mentioned. Use the tools to see what you can learn about Jericho. Let the class continue to work in their groups of four to six. Circulate among the groups to help where needed. After the groups have had enough time to find much of the material, let the groups share. It is easy to see how the use of Bible study tools plus your teacher's book can help you to be prepared for an interesting Bible lesson.

Now, evaluate your own study habits. Use the chart in Chapter Four in Teach With Success. *Rate yourself.* (Allow time for this. Have each person work individually.)

Expand *(10 minutes)*

Look back at those original questions with which we started. Would you change any answers now? When we teach the Bible, we have a special job given to us by God.

So how will you get to know your subject? There are many ways to get to know the Bible well. Let's work on making a five-point plan for knowing the subject. Decide on five things which would lead you to be adequately prepared. Put them in their order of importance. After you have developed your personal plan for study, share your plan with your group members. Plan time for individual work, then for group discussion. Have each group close by praying specifically for one another.

Execute

1. Read Chapter Five in *Teach With Success*.
2. Use Bible study tools to find what you can about the Nazarites. Write your report and turn it in to the teacher next week.

3. Choose a Bible lesson for an age group of your choice. Follow each preparation step suggested in the teacher's book. Be ready to share with class members next week how you did in your personal discipline to prepare.

LESSON 5

Know How To Teach

Goals: Each pupil should be able to:
1. *Define* teaching in his own words.
2. *List* nine rules of teaching.
3. *Illustrate* each of the nine rules of teaching.
4. *List* nine indicators of good teaching.
5. *Evaluate* a teacher whom he observes to determine which of the rules of teaching are being used.
6. *Plan* a Bible lesson using the nine rules of teaching.

Materials: Magazines, shelf paper, glue or paste, felt pens, posterboard, pencils, Bibles, poster or overhead transparency containing the nine rules of teaching, index cards.

Excite *(ET plus 15 minutes)*

As each pupil arrives, give him a piece of paper which says, "Teaching is . . ." with instructions to make at least five completions for the sentence. After the pupil has completed the sentence he may choose one of three activities to illustrate what teaching is. Activity possibilities: 1) a montage in which a series of pictures tells a story or carries out a theme, 2) a song, and 3) a picture wheel. After the activities are finished, let the groups share what they did.

Review Colossians 1:9, 10 as an outline for Bible teaching: facts, understanding, behavior, and service. Remind the pupils that this cycle of learning is essential.

TRANSITION SENTENCES: *Teaching is communicating God's Word in order to change lives. Today we will discuss the nine rules of teaching so that we can learn to teach well.*

Explain *(25 minutes)*

Display a chart or an overhead transparency which shows the nine rules of teaching mentioned in Chapter Five. Read the list, illustrating each rule as you go.

Let's see how Jesus used the rules of teaching. Turn to Matthew 13:1-23. We will divide into groups to learn how Jesus used each rule. Divide the class into nine groups. Or if the class is small, individuals may work on each rule.

1. *Know what is taught.* Jesus knew the subject matter since He is the Son of God.
2. *Know what changes in behavior you are seeking.* It appears that Jesus was seeking people who would grow in the kingdom.
3. *Gain attention.* He used a common story.
4. *Use words understood in the same way by both teachers and pupils.* Note the simplicity of Jesus' vocabulary.
5. *Lead the pupil from the known to the unknown.* Jesus again used the commonplace.
6. *Stimulate the pupil's mind to action.* See verses 9, 10.
7. *Actively involve the learners.* They listened to real-life material.
8. *Require the pupil to reproduce the lesson.* See verse 9. He eventually called His pupils to follow Him, too.
9. *Repeat and review.* Note verses 18-23. Let the groups report. If they miss any pertinent information, fill it in.

Explore *(20 minutes)*

Let's suppose you are assigned to teach a class of third and fourth graders about the prodigal son in

Luke 15:11-32. How would you try to use the nine rules of teaching as you prepared and taught? Remember what third and fourth graders are like. You won't have time to completely prepare a lesson, of course, but you can begin to think about how to use the rules. Divide the class into pairs who will make preliminary plans about how to use the rules to teach Luke 15:11-32 to third and fourth graders. Let them share after they have finished. Make any necessary corrections or additions.

Expand *(10 minutes)*

How can you check up on your teaching? How can you tell if you are, in fact, communicating effectively? Your pupils will give you some indicators. What would those be? Lead a brief discussion letting the pupils suggest the indicators. List them on the chalkboard. Add any others mentioned in *Teach With Success:* interest, participation, attendance, activity, flexibility, realism purpose, problem-solving, and behavior.

Why not check yourself then? At the end of Chapter Five, you will find a chart "How To Teach Better." Look it over. Decide which is your pattern. Then look back over your evaluation. Where do you need to go to work? What will you do first? Put your list on the index card you will be given and commit yourself now to do something about it. Allow time. Conclude with prayer.

Execute

1. Read Chapter Six in *Teach With Success.*
2. Observe a class. Did the teacher use the rules of teaching? With what success? What indicators of pupil interest did you see?
3. If you teach a class this week, evaluate yourself in the same way as you did when you observed.

LESSON 6

Know Your Room and Equipment

Goals: Each pupil should be able to:
1. *Identify* the optimum size for each age level department.
2. *List* the desirable features of a classroom for each age level.
3. *Evaluate* specific classroom facilities as to desirable features and needed improvement.
4. *Make a plan* for improving a specific class or department facility.

Materials: Chart or overhead transparency showing desirable classroom sizes for each age group, diagrams showing arrangement for preschool classes, checklists for rooms and equipment, pencils, overhead transparency with **agree/disagree** statements.

Excite *(ET plus 20 minutes)*

As the pupils arrive, have the overhead projector set up with a transparency featuring the following statements. Have students mark **agree** or **disagree** for each one on a separate sheet of paper.

1. Rooms and equipment are not important in a Sunday school.
2. Adults need more space than children since they are bigger.
3. An effective teacher will do a good job regardless of the physical facilities in which he teaches.
4. The best building arrangement is for classrooms to be small. That way no class will be too large for a teacher to handle.
5. Chalkboards and bulletin boards should be at the eye level of the pupils.
6. Chairs and tables need to be the right size for the pupils.
7. It isn't really important to provide teaching materials for a teacher. A good teacher will be creative enough to come up with ideas on his own.

After the pupils have finished the **agree/disagree** list, discuss each question. Allow individuals to express why they answered as they did.

Divide the class into debate groups. The issue is: Resolved: Churches must be concerned about and provide adequate teaching facilities and equipment. One group may develop their argument for the issue, the other an argument against. Take a few minutes to present the arguments.

TRANSITION SENTENCES: *Of course, good teachers can do an effective job in less-than-adequate facilities; but learning and teaching are far more pleasant in an appropriate setting. Let's find out how to have good facilities.*

Explain (15 minutes)

Go over the criteria for good classrooms presented in Chapter Six. Use a chart or an overhead transparency to outline classroom sizes (square footage per pupil) for each age group. You may wish to use similar visuals to present all of the criteria. Spend some time showing how preschool classrooms may be arranged to use interest centers effectively. It would be helpful to have diagrams duplicated for distribution at this time.

Explore (20 minutes)

If your building is relatively small and if the training class is few in number, take a group tour of the building and equipment available for teaching. If either your building or class is large, divide into four groups. Let one group evaluate facilities and equipment for preschoolers, another group for children, another for youth, and another for adults. Each group should tour the facilities, using the inventory sheet at the end of Chapter Six. A different inventory sheet will be needed for each department or class. Each group should come back with a description of what they saw plus evaluative comments about the strengths and weaknesses of each area. Allow time for the reports.

Expand (10-15 minutes)

How could our building and equipment be improved? Was everything perfect as you saw it? If not, how could it be made better? Work in your groups to devise a plan to improve the facilities you observed. What needs to be done to have top-notch facilities? In what order should these be done? Put these in a priority ranking. What could be done with minimal expenditure of money? What could the teacher do? What would have to await official action? Let the groups work on this problem. Then take time for quick reports.

Finish the class session by challenging the pupils to do what they can do themselves to improve their classrooms. Have a time of prayer.

Execute

1. Read Chapter Seven in *Teach With Success*.
2. If you are teaching, evaluate your own classroom. Evaluate its strengths and weaknesses. What needs to be done to this room? In what order should these things be done? Put them in priority ranking. Pick one task to begin to do *this week*. If you aren't teaching now, do the same for the meeting room for the class which you attend. Share your findings with your teacher.

LESSON 7

Follow A Plan

Goals: Each pupil should be able to:
1. *State* at least three reasons why lesson planning is important for a teacher.
2. *List* the essential components of an effective Bible lesson.
3. *Cite* examples of how to implement each part of the Bible lesson.
4. *Choose* appropriate teaching aims.

5. *Plan* an effective Bible lesson, using a curriculum quarterly as a guide.

Materials: A teacher's quarterly for each age level, pencils, paper, Bibles, road maps, blueprints, diagrams for putting something together, overhead transparency or handout or poster of a lesson plan.

Excite (ET plus 15 minutes)

Before the pupils arrive, write on the chalkboard, "To fail to plan is to plan to fail." Then as the pupils arrive, assign each to a group to plan a trip from your community to some point of your choice seven hundred miles away. What routes will they take? How long will it take to make the trip? Should the trip be made in one day or two? Where would an overnight stop be made if it is to be a two-day trip? Are there any special things to see on the way? Are there any special cautions to be observed? Let the groups work out the itinerary. Then let them share with the rest of the class. Compare their plans.

It is interesting to plan a trip. Even though the planned itinerary need not be inflexible when we have finished with it, planning helps us to use our travel time wisely and to see everything we want to see along the way.

Blueprints and construction diagrams are plans, too. Show some. Explain how they are used if the class doesn't know.

TRANSITION SENTENCES: *A lesson plan is like a road map or a blueprint or a construction diagram. It helps us to decide how to achieve our goal for teaching. When we learn to make and follow a plan, we are on our way to becoming successful teachers.*

Explain (20 minutes)

A lesson is seldom taught in isolation from all other lessons. Lesson materials usually present materials in units consisting of three to six lessons which are related in some way. For example, you may have four lessons dealing with sin. Each lesson will contribute to the overall theme. You need to first look at your materials as a whole to see how lessons relate to each other. Illustrate from the curriculum materials.

Go over the steps for preparing a lesson. Illustrate by showing a lesson in a teacher's quarterly. Put the lesson plan form in this book on an overhead transparency and/or handouts to be distributed to the pupils. Explain and illustrate the objective, hook to the lesson, book (or Bible study), look (or application), and took (the commitment to action). Explain and illustrate each part.

Explore and Expand (30 minutes)

Let's try it. Let's see how we can do in preparing a Bible lesson. Suppose you are assigned to teach a lesson using Luke 15:11-32. Divide the class into groups to plan a lesson for an age group of its choice. The groups won't finish this, of course. But help them to get started, and let them know that they will have opportunity to finish the assignment individually before next week. Questions to be dealt with are:

1. What is this Bible passage saying?
2. What is the Bible saying that is important and understandable for the age group you teach? Your class? Particular individuals in the class?
3. Write a lesson objective. Make it clear-short-specific.
4. Decide on three possible hooks.
5. Decide on the main points of the Bible study and three ways to present them.
6. Decide on the main points of the application and three ways to do the look.
7. Decide on three ways to do the took. When the class time is over, lead a closing prayer.

Execute

1. Read Chapter Eight in *Teach With Success.*
2. Finish planning the lesson you began in today's class session. See how many methods of impression in Chapter Eight you can incorporate into the lesson.
3. Prepare an assigned method of impression to report and demonstrate to the class. Be ready to describe the method, suggest ways to use it, and then give a brief demonstration.

LESSON 8

Use Methods of Impression

Goals: Each pupil should be able to:
1. *Distinguish* between methods of impression and expression.
2. *List* at least ten methods of impression.
3. *Prepare* at least ten methods of impression.
4. *Plan* to use at least three methods of impression in a Bible lesson.

Materials: Paper, pencils, Bibles.

Excite *(ET plus 10 minutes)*

As the pupils arrive, give them a sheet of paper with the following instructions: *Draw a boat large enough to house people and animals.* Let the pupils work on the assignment. Then let them show their work.

Was it easy to know exactly what to draw? Why? Lead the discussion to the point where the pupils acknowledge the difficulty since large is a relative term, there are many kinds of boats, and the number of animals was not defined. If they had seen a picture beforehand, it would have been an easier task for them. Show them a picture or give them a diagram and have them do it again. Share the results. This should demonstrate the importance of using visuals to impress our teaching upon the minds of the pupils.

TRANSITION SENTENCES: *Visuals help us to teach. And it is true, a visual is really worth a thousand words. Let's see the wide variety of visuals available for us to use.*

Explain and Explore *(45 minutes)*

Have the pupils make their reports and demonstrations on the methods of impression outlined in Chapter Eight. Add any necessary information which a reporter may omit.

Expand *(5 minutes)*

Which methods of impression have you used? Which ones should you use more often? Check yourself on it. Turn to the last page in Chapter Eight and rate yourself. Then when you are finished pick one method to consider using the next time you teach.

Execute

1. Read Chapter Nine from *Teach With Success.*
2. Decide how you could use two or three methods of expression in the Bible lesson you have planned.
3. Prepare a report and demonstration of a method of expression as assigned by the teacher. Each report-demonstration should describe the method, suggest how to use it, and briefly demonstrate its proper use.

LESSON 9

Use Methods of Expression

Goals: Each pupil should be able to:
1. *List* ten methods of pupil expression for teaching.
2. *Demonstrate* the use of one method of pupil expression.
3. *Plan* to use two or three methods of expression in the Bible lesson already planned.
4. *Select* the best methods for a particular lesson.

Materials: Shelf paper, felt pens, and chart.

Excite (ET plus 10 minutes)

Place a piece of shelf paper or table paper on the wall before the pupils arrive. Place the words "I learn best when . . ." on it. As the pupils arrive, have them write their responses on the graffiti chart. Then assign them to groups of five or six to discuss the following question: "How many ways can you think of to actively involve pupils in a Bible lesson?" After the groups have had time to adequately cover the question, let them share their answers. List suggestions on the chalkboard. Go over the responses on the graffiti chart.

TRANSITION SENTENCES: *People learn more and remember longer when they are actively involved in the learning process. So let's find out 18 ways to involve pupils in learning.*

Explain and Explore (45 minutes)

Have the pupils make their reports and demonstrations on the methods of expression outlined in Chapter Nine. Add any necessary information which a reporter may miss.

Outline the material from "How to Select the Method to Be Used" in Chapter Nine, using a poster to visualize them.

Expand (5 minutes)

How well do you involve your pupils in learning? Check yourself by filling out the chart on the last page of Chapter Nine. Then choose one method to use the first opportunity you have. Close with prayer.

Execute

1. Read Chapter Ten in *Teach With Success.*
2. Observe a children's class, either at church or school. What behavior problems did you see? Why do you think they arose? Could something have been done to prevent the problem? Was the problem handled appropriately?

LESSON 10

Maintain Classroom Control

Goals: Each pupil should be able to:
1. *List* the common causes of classroom behavior challenges.
2. *Suggest* solutions for classroom behavior challenges.
3. *Identify* tentative causes for classroom behavior challenges when they occur.
4. *Confidently handle* a classroom situation.

Materials: Cartoon cards to illustrate how to correct behavior.

Excite (ET plus 10 minutes)

Have nothing prepared for the pupils to do as they arrive today. Offer no suggestions at all; let them entertain themselves. When you are ready to begin the session, ask four or five pupils to role play the following classroom situation.

A junior class of boys and girls stream in on Sunday morning. The teacher, Mr. (or Mrs.) Smith has no opening activities planned for the students as they arrive. (He is too busy reading the teaching materials.) When Mr. Smith is finally ready to start the class, behavior difficulties emerge. Flustered, he becomes cold and vindictive.

Discuss what happened.
1. What problems did you see?
2. What caused the problems you observed?
3. Did the teacher handle the problems well?
4. How could he have handled the problems more effectively?

Discuss how they reacted to your beginning today.

TRANSITION SENTENCES: *Getting the pupils' attention at the beginning of a class is essential, whatever the age. It can make the difference between success and failure. But there are other things we need to know to have good discipline.*

Explain (25 minutes)

Divide the class into five buzz groups of equal numbers in each group. Give each group a different cause for discipline problems—physical conditions, emotional climate, home, the child himself, and instructional planning. Instruct them to list as many causes of discipline problems as possible for the category. If there is time, have them suggest solutions. Let the groups report back.

Go over the rules for correcting misbehavior, illustrating each with examples and cartoon cards.

Explore (25 minutes)

Let's use the principles we have suggested. The buzz groups may work to solve the following cases.

1. A class of kindergarteners has twelve children and one teacher. The teacher wasn't there when the children began to arrive. Tommy, who is shy, has been to Sunday school only a few times before. When he arrives, he begins to cry. The crying becomes louder and louder as the morning progresses. What is the problem? What preventive measures should have been taken? What can be done to correct the situation?

2. Shelly and Miriam are second graders who like to talk. When they sit beside each other, they talk all of the time. Today they keep interrupting the teacher when they aren't talking to each other. What is the problem? What preventive measures should have been taken? What corrective measures can be taken?

3. Mr. Jones teaches a Junior High class. In an effort to cover all of the material in the teacher's quarterly, he does most of the talk-ing. Some of his pupils sit and talk to each other. Some are apathetic. Some talk aloud. What is the problem? What preventive measures could Mr. Jones take? What corrective measures?

4. A class of twos and threes becomes restless every Sunday and refuses to sit still. What is the problem? What preventive measures should have been taken? What corrective measures can be taken?

5. Brian is much brighter than all of the other fourth graders. He usually doesn't want to do what everyone else does, and when he does, he finishes first. He is not at all cooperative. What is the problem? What preventive measures should have been taken? What corrective measures can be taken?

Allow sufficient time for discussion, then ask for reports. Invite any additional discussion.

Expand (5 minutes)

Check yourself now, especially what kind of emotional climate you establish. Turn to the section "Cause of Discipline Problems." Work your way through the five causes and rate yourself and your teaching. Do the same for how you correct a problem. Then decide the one area you need most to work on. Close with prayer.

Execute

1. Read Chapter Eleven in *Teach With Success*.
2. Interview four or five teachers. Ask "How do you evaluate yourself and your pupils? How do you know you are accomplishing what you want to accomplish?"

LESSON 11

Evaluate Your Pupils

Goals: Each pupil should be able to:
1. *Define* evaluation.
2. *List* four reasons for evaluation of pupils.
3. *List* four ways to evaluate pupils in his class.
4. *Determine* the growth of the pupils in his class.

5. *Commit* himself to utilize at least one method for continuous evaluation of the pupils in his class.

Materials: Cake, woodworking project, sheet of newsprint, felt pen, index cards, pencils.

Excite (ET plus 15 minutes)

As the pupils arrive, serve them cake. Let them eat it. Then ask, "Was this good cake?" Let them answer. Then ask, "How do you know it was a good cake?" Let the pupils suggest answers. List their answers on the chalkboard.

Next, show the pupils a well-made hand designed woodworking project. Ask, "Is this a well-made object?" Allow responses. Then ask, "How do you know?" Let the pupils suggest criteria. List these on the chalkboard.

TRANSITION SENTENCES: *We have just made two evaluations. We determined the quality of a cake and a woodworking project. In much the same way we must evaluate our teaching. The big difference is that our product is a person, not an object.*

Explain (30 minutes)

Why is it important to evaluate? Why not just teach and let it go at that? Have the pupils suggest reasons to evaluate teaching. List the reasons on a sheet of newsprint. Add anything appropriate not suggested by the pupils.

How may we evaluate? What indicators or criteria tell us that the pupils are growing? Let's see if we can think of some ways. Let the pupils work in small groups—one for preschoolers, one for children, one for youth, one for adults. *List any criteria we can use to determine whether or not the pupil is learning. Then try to select ways to get that data.* After the groups have worked on this, let them make reports to the class as a whole. Record ideas on the newsprint. *Obviously, there are many ways to evaluate besides giving tests.*

A good way to evaluate continuously is to keep a notebook page on each pupil. A good example is at the end of Chapter Eleven. (Look it over.)

Explore (5 minutes)

Give each pupil an index card. *Let's see how this works. Choose one pupil from the class you teach or attend. Using the criteria for the age level of the person you have chosen, evaluate his spiritual development. Jot down your notes on the index card you were given.*

Expand (5 minutes)

Keep that card with you. As you gain other data, jot it down. Be alert for evaluation opportunities so you can continue to teach so pupils may grow. Close with prayer.

Execute

1. Read Chapter Twelve in *Teach With Success.*
2. Continue to collect evaluation data for the pupil whom you chose.
3. Distribute the teacher evaluation form in your class if you teach.

LESSON 12

Evaluate Your Teaching

Goals: Each pupil should be able to:
1. **List** criteria by which he evaluates the effectiveness of his teaching.
2. **Determine,** on the basis of the criteria, his effectiveness in teaching.
3. **Select** an area in which to work to improve his effectiveness.

Materials: Pencils, index cards.

Excite (ET plus 15 minutes)

As the pupils arrive, give them index cards with this sentence on them: "I know I have taught well when . . ." Have the pupils form groups of three to draw up a list of criteria by which they feel confident their teaching has been done well. Caution them not to make this an evaluation of pupil responses. It is, instead, an assessment of what the teacher did. After the groups have drawn up their lists, combine the results in a master list of criteria. Discuss the criteria.

Explain and Explore (35 minutes)

TRANSITION SENTENCES: *Today is an evaluation session. We have now drawn up a system of evaluation for ourselves. So let's evaluate our teaching. Only you know how well you do, so we will let you evaluate.*

1. *Your lesson plan.* Check yourself on the chart at the beginning of the chapter. As you do, jot down at the bottom of the page one thing you need to work on.
2. *Your classroom.* Use the chart on page 131 to evaluate your environment. At the bottom of the page, write down one thing you need to work on right away.
3. *Your voice qualities.* Use the chart on page 132 to evaluate your voice usage. In the space provided, write down one thing you need to work on right away.
4. *Your classroom interaction.* Go over the form on page 135 to show what kind of evaluation is important.
5. *Student's evaluation of the class.* Have pupils

report on their results of giving this device to others.

Continuous evaluation of ourselves as teachers is essential. Make sure you do it, and you will become an increasingly effective teacher.

Expand (10 minutes)

Now go back to each of the things you picked out to work on in your own teaching procedures. Look over the three. Put them in order of priority on the back of the index card you used earlier. Then put down two specific actions you will begin now to take to accomplish those goals. After you have done that, share your commitment with the others in your earlier group of three. Close with prayer in your group.

Execute

1. Read Chapter Thirteen in *Teach With Success.*
2. Teach a lesson. Grade yourself using the chart at the end of Chapter Twelve. (If you do not teach a class, the instructor will give you a teaching assignment.)

LESSON 13

Evaluate Yourself

Goals: Each pupil should be able to:
1. *Cite* Scriptural guidelines which outline his responsibility and qualifications as a teacher.
2. *Determine* how well he meets the Biblical criteria for teaching.
3. *Develop* a plan for improvement as a teacher.
4. *Commit* himself to be a teacher.

Materials: Bibles, pencils, newsprint, felt pens, Plasti-Tak, index cards.

Excite (ET plus 10 minutes)

As the pupils arrive, ask them to complete the "My Job and I" chart at the beginning of Chapter Thirteen. Have them tally up their score and record the number (no identification is necessary) on the

chalkboard. Discuss the scores and what they show. Encourage pupils to talk about how they respond to that evaluation.

Explain (25 minutes)

TRANSITION SENTENCES: *How do you rate? How well are you doing? The best way to evaluate oneself is to use God's Word as the standard for measuring. Let's do that.*

Divide the class into five groups, each group studying Scriptures relating to a different facet of teaching. Each group will also receive a felt pen and a sheet of newsprint on which to write evaluation questions based on the Scriptures studied.

1. Purpose—Matthew 28:19, 20; Ephesians 4:12, 13.
2. Qualifications—2 Timothy 2:2; James 3; Titus 1:9.
3. Lesson Preparation—2 Corinthians 4:7; 1 Timothy 4:16; Hebrews 5:12-14; 2 Peter 3:18; 2 Timothy 2:15.
4. Lesson Presentation—2 Timothy 2:14, 16-18, 21-26; 1 Timothy 3:5; 2 Timothy 4:1-5; 1 Corinthians 16:14; 2 Peter 1:16-21; Acts 7:2; 22:3; 26:2, 29.
5. Final Grade—James 3:1; Romans 2:12; 1 Timothy 4:16. Let the groups report their findings.

Explore (10 minutes)

How well do you measure up? Take your index card and evaluate yourself in these five areas. What do you need to do next? How can you improve?

Expand (15 minutes)

What have we learned during these past thirteen weeks? What do you think is the most important thing we have learned? Go around the classroom until everyone has answered. *What do you feel you need to do most to be the kind of teacher God wants you to be?* Again go around the classroom until everyone has answered.

Teaching is the most exciting job God could ever give. Surely He could have chosen an infallible means of communicating His Word—but He chose us. Let's join together in the great adventure of teaching! Close with prayer.

Execute

1. Teach!
2. Teach well!
3. Teach to glorify God!

Resources

Bolton, Barbara, and Smith, Charles T. *Bible Learning Activities—Children*. Glendale, California: Regal Press, 1972.

Bolton, Barbara, and Smith, Charles T. *Creative Bible Learning—Children*. Glendale, California: Regal Press, 1977.

Campbell, Patsy, Lang, June, and Eynon, Dana. *77 Dynamic Ideas for Teaching the Bible to Children*. Cincinnati: Standard Publishing, 1977.

Dickinson, Dean. *Help! I've Got Problems! for Adult teachers and leaders*. Cincinnati: Standard Publishing, 1978.

Edge, Findley B. *Teach for Results*. Nashville: Broadman Press, 1956.

Edge, Findley B. *Helping the Teacher*. Nashville: Broadman Press, 1959.

Gregory, John Milton. *The Seven Laws of Teaching*. Grand Rapids: Baker, 1954.

Gronlund, Norman. *Stating Behavioral Objectives for Classroom Instruction*. New York: MacMillan, 1970.

Harrell, Donna, and Haystead, Wes. *Creative Bible Learning—Birth-5 Years*. Glendale, California: Regal Press, 1977.

Leypoldt, Martha. *40 Ways To Teach In Groups*. Valley Forge, Pennsylvania: Judson, 1967.

Leypoldt, Martha. *Learning Is Change*. Valley Forge, Pennsylvania: Judson, 1971.

Marlowe, Monroe, and Reed, Bobbie. *Creative Bible Learning—Adults*. Glendale, California: Regal Press, 1977.

McKinley, Richard, and Baynes, Richard. *77 Dynamic Ideas for Teaching the Bible to Adults*. Cincinnati: Standard Publishing, 1977.

Mobley, Ron. *Help! I've Got Problems! for Teen teachers and leaders*. Cincinnati: Standard Publishing, 1978.

Odor, Ruth. *Help! I've Got Problems! for Children's teachers and leaders*. Cincinnati: Standard Publishing, 1978.

Pierson, James. *77 Dynamic Ideas for the Christian Education of the Handicapped*. Cincinnati: Standard Publishing, 1977.

Reed, Bobbie, and Reed, Ed. *Creative Bible Learning—Youth*. Glendale, California: Regal Press, 1977.

Richards, Lawrence O. *Creative Bible Teaching*. Chicago: Moody Press, 1970.

Skaugset, Arlene, and Short, Loretta. *Help! I've Got Problems! for Preschool teachers and leaders*. Cincinnati: Standard Publishing, 1978.

Stortz, Diane, and Shaffer, Wilma. *77 Dynamic Ideas for Teaching the Bible to Pre-Schoolers*. Cincinnati: Standard Publishing, 1977.

Trotter, Judy, and Curie, Barbara. *77 Dynamic Ideas for Teaching the Bible to Teens*. Cincinnati: Standard Publishing, 1977.

Zuck, Roy. *Spiritual Power in Your Teaching*. Chicago: Moody Press, 1963.